Copyright © 2023 by Sophia M. Johnson (Author)

All rights reserved. This book or any portion thereof may not be reproduced or used in any manner whatsoever without the express written permission of the publisher except for the use of brief quotations in a book review.

This book is copyright protected. This is only for personal use. You cannot amend, distributor, sell, use, quote or paraphrase any part or the content within this book without the consent of the author.

Please note the information contained within this document is for educational and entertainment purposes only. Every attempt has been made to provide accurate, up to date and reliable complete information. No warranties of any kind are expressed or implied. Readers acknowledge that the author is not engaging in the rendering of legal, financial, medical or professional advice. The content of this book has been derived from various sources. Please consult a licensed professional before attempting any techniques outlined in this book.

By reading this document, the readers agree that under no circumstances are the author responsible for any losses, direct or indirect, which are incurred as a result of the use of information contained within this document, including but not limited to errors, omissions or inaccuracies.

Thank you very much for reading this book.

Table of Contents

History of Christmas Eve Movie Traditions

'Tis the season for festive lights, joyful carols, and the warm embrace of beloved Christmas movies that have become an integral part of our holiday traditions. As we embark on this cinematic journey through the enchanting world of Christmas Eve classics, it's essential to understand the rich history and enduring traditions that have shaped the way we celebrate the holiday season.

The origins of watching movies on Christmas Eve trace back to a time when families sought heartwarming and entertaining ways to come together and usher in the festive spirit. While Christmas itself has deep-rooted traditions of gift-giving, feasting, and caroling, the inclusion of movies as part of the celebration emerged more gradually.

In the early 20th century, the emergence of the film industry coincided with a growing desire for shared experiences during the holiday season. Theaters began screening special Christmas-themed films, providing an opportunity for families and friends to gather and immerse themselves in the magic of storytelling. These cinematic experiences quickly became a cherished part of the Christmas Eve festivities.

As technology advanced and television sets found their way into households across the globe, the tradition of Christmas Eve movie watching evolved. Families would huddle around their living room screens, eagerly anticipating the annual broadcast of classic holiday films. This transition from theaters to living rooms marked a shift in the way people engaged with Christmas Eve movies but did not diminish the significance of these cinematic traditions.

The 1940s and 1950s witnessed the emergence of timeless classics such as "It's a Wonderful Life," a film that would go on to redefine the Christmas movie genre. Frank Capra's masterpiece not only encapsulated the spirit of Christmas but also set a precedent for the enduring themes and values that would characterize many Christmas Eve classics to come.

Throughout the decades, the concept of a Christmas Eve movie marathon gained popularity. Families started curating their own lists of must-watch films, creating a unique blend of nostalgia, laughter, and heartwarming moments. The ritual of watching these movies became a shared experience, fostering a sense of togetherness and unity during the festive season.

The 1980s and 1990s brought forth a new wave of Christmas classics that catered to diverse tastes and sensibilities. From the slapstick humor of "Home Alone" to the poignant lessons of "A Christmas Carol," filmmakers explored different genres while staying true to the essence of Christmas storytelling. This era solidified the notion that there was a Christmas movie for everyone, regardless of age or background.

In recent years, the advent of streaming services has further transformed how we engage with Christmas Eve movies. The ability to access a vast library of films at the touch of a button has given audiences unprecedented choice and flexibility in curating their holiday watchlists. However, the enduring appeal of the classics remains, with many turning to the familiar warmth of these time-honored films to create a sense of continuity and tradition in an ever-changing world.

As we delve into the chapters that explore the nuances of iconic Christmas Eve classics, let us reflect on the evolution of these traditions. From the early days of cinematic magic to the present era of on-demand streaming, the history of Christmas Eve movie traditions is a testament to the timeless allure of storytelling and the enduring power of the holiday spirit. So, grab a cup of cocoa, gather your loved ones, and join us on this journey through the heartwarming, hilarious, and sometimes unexpected tales that have become synonymous with Christmas Eve celebrations.

As we embark on this cinematic exploration of Christmas Eve classics, it is essential to delve into the very essence that infuses these films with timeless charm—the intangible yet palpable spirit of Christmas. Beyond the twinkling lights, festive decorations, and jolly melodies, the Christmas spirit encapsulates a profound sense of joy, generosity, and goodwill towards all. In this chapter, we will unravel the nuances of this elusive but enchanting force that permeates the narratives of our favorite holiday films.

The Christmas spirit is an ethereal concept that transcends cultural boundaries, uniting people in a shared celebration of joy, love, and hope. It is a season when hearts seem to grow warmer, and a collective desire to spread happiness becomes a guiding force. But what exactly constitutes the Christmas spirit, and how do our beloved Christmas Eve classics capture and embody this essence?

At its core, the Christmas spirit is a celebration of generosity and selflessness. It is a time when individuals are inspired to give rather than receive, to extend a helping hand to those in need, and to foster a sense of community. This spirit is beautifully encapsulated in the narratives of many Christmas movies, where characters undergo transformative journeys that reflect the universal themes of love, redemption, and the power of human connection.

The quintessential Christmas movie becomes a vessel for these timeless values, serving as a reminder that the holiday season is not just about presents under the tree but about the intangible gifts of kindness, compassion, and understanding. Whether it's George Bailey learning the true worth of his life in "It's a Wonderful Life" or Scrooge's redemption in "A Christmas Carol," these stories echo the sentiment that the true magic of Christmas lies in the goodness we share with others.

Furthermore, the Christmas spirit is intricately tied to the concept of nostalgia. The holiday season has a unique ability to transport us back to cherished memories of childhood, family gatherings, and the simple joys of festive traditions. Christmas movies often leverage this powerful connection to nostalgia, using familiar settings, heartwarming scenarios, and iconic symbols to evoke a sense of warmth and familiarity. Through the lens of these films, audiences are transported to a world where the magic of Christmas is not just a fleeting moment but a timeless, enduring presence.

In examining the Christmas spirit within the context of our outlined Christmas Eve classics, we witness how each film contributes to the broader tapestry of this festive emotion. For instance, "Elf" embodies the exuberance and childlike wonder that characterizes the holiday season, portraying a character who brings unbridled joy to everyone he encounters. On the other hand, "A Christmas Carol" confronts the darker aspects of human nature, illustrating how redemption and compassion can triumph over greed and selfishness, ultimately capturing the transformative power inherent in the Christmas spirit.

The Christmas spirit is also expressed through the communal aspects of the holiday season. Families coming together, communities sharing in festivities, and strangers extending acts of kindness—all these elements contribute to the collective experience of joy that defines Christmas. In movies like "Christmas Vacation," the chaotic but ultimately heartwarming portrayal of a family's holiday gathering resonates with audiences who recognize the imperfect yet precious nature of their own celebrations.

As we traverse through the narratives of "Love Actually," the interconnected stories reveal the diverse ways people experience love and connection during the holiday season. The film becomes a testament to the idea that, in the midst of the hustle and bustle, it is the relationships we cultivate and cherish that truly embody the spirit of Christmas.

The Christmas spirit, as depicted in our Christmas Eve classics, is not confined to a singular narrative or expression. It manifests in various forms—be it the whimsical humor of "The Grinch" or the hauntingly beautiful fantasy of "The Polar Express." The underlying thread, however, remains consistent: a celebration of the human spirit, the capacity for transformation, and the enduring power of love and kindness.

In conclusion, as we immerse ourselves in the enchanting worlds of our chosen Christmas Eve classics, let us remain attuned to the heartbeat of the holiday season—the Christmas spirit. Through the lens of these films, we discover that beyond the tinsel and mistletoe, it is the universal themes of love, generosity, and shared humanity that truly define the magic of Christmas. So, as we journey through these cinematic wonders, may the Christmas spirit illuminate our hearts and remind us of the enduring joy that comes from embracing the true meaning of the season.

Greatest Christmas Movies Criteria

As we embark on a festive odyssey through the annals of Christmas Eve cinema, it's imperative to establish the criteria by which we measure the greatness of these holiday films. What makes a Christmas movie truly exceptional? Is it the ability to evoke laughter, stir emotions, or impart timeless lessons? In this segment, we delve into the parameters that define the greatness of our chosen Christmas classics, setting the stage for a discerning exploration of their impact on the holiday tradition.

Defining the greatest Christmas movies involves navigating a delicate balance between personal sentiment and broader cultural impact. While individual preferences certainly play a role in determining the 'greatness' of a film, certain universal criteria emerge as guiding lights in this cinematic winter wonderland.

Timelessness: Great Christmas movies possess an enduring quality that transcends temporal boundaries. They stand the test of time, becoming cherished classics that resonate across generations. Consider "It's a Wonderful Life," a film that has not only weathered the decades but continues to captivate audiences with its timeless themes of love, community, and the profound impact of a single life.

Emotional Resonance: At the heart of every great Christmas movie lies the ability to elicit genuine emotional responses. Whether it's tears of joy, laughter, or a tug at the heartstrings, these films possess a unique alchemy that forges a deep connection with viewers. "Love Actually" navigates the complex terrain of love and relationships, weaving a tapestry of emotions that mirrors the diverse experiences of the holiday season.

Inspirational Messages: The greatest Christmas movies often convey messages that extend beyond the screen, imparting valuable lessons about love, kindness, and the true spirit of the season. "A Christmas Carol" is a prime example, using the transformative journey of Ebenezer Scrooge to underscore the importance of compassion and generosity—a lesson that reverberates far beyond the confines of Victorian London.

Iconic Characters: Memorable characters are the lifeblood of great Christmas movies. From the mischievous Kevin McCallister in "Home Alone" to the whimsical Buddy in "Elf," these characters etch themselves into our collective consciousness, becoming enduring symbols of the holiday season. The resonance of these characters contributes significantly to the cultural legacy of the films.

Cinematic Craftsmanship: While the holiday season exudes a certain whimsy, the craftsmanship behind the camera is a crucial aspect of a great Christmas movie. Technical achievements, storytelling prowess, and visual splendor collectively elevate these films into the realm of cinematic excellence. "The Polar Express" stands out not only for its groundbreaking motion capture but also for its immersive visual spectacle that transports audiences to a magical winter wonderland.

Versatility and Appeal: The greatest Christmas movies have a universal appeal that transcends demographic boundaries. Whether you're a child enchanted by the magic of "The Nightmare Before Christmas" or an adult reveling in the nostalgia of "A Christmas Story," these films cater to a broad audience, fostering a sense of shared celebration.

Impact on Popular Culture: The mark of a truly great Christmas movie is its enduring impact on popular culture. These films become ingrained in the holiday zeitgeist, influencing traditions, inspiring references, and even shaping the cultural lexicon. "Christmas Vacation" has not only become synonymous with over-the-top holiday celebrations but has also left an indelible mark on the broader landscape of Christmas comedy.

Lasting Legacy: A great Christmas movie stands the test of time, not just in terms of its ongoing popularity but also in its ability to shape and contribute to the broader Christmas movie landscape. Whether it's "How the Grinch Stole Christmas" inspiring subsequent adaptations or "A Christmas Carol" influencing countless retellings, the lasting legacy of these films is a testament to their greatness.

In navigating the criteria that define the greatest Christmas movies, we embark on a journey that transcends personal preferences and delves into the collective experience of the holiday season. These films, each a unique snowflake in the cinematic blizzard of Christmas Eve classics, weave a tapestry of joy, laughter, and timeless lessons. As we immerse ourselves in their narratives, let us keep these criteria in mind, guiding us through the enchanting landscapes of holiday magic that define the greatest Christmas movies of all time.

Chapter 1 - It's a Wonderful Life (1946)
Timeless Storytelling and Themes

In the grand tapestry of Christmas Eve classics, few films shine as brightly as the timeless masterpiece, "It's a Wonderful Life." Directed by the visionary Frank Capra and released in 1946, this cinematic gem has not only endured the passage of time but has ingrained itself into the very soul of the holiday season. As we unravel the layers of this cinematic treasure, we begin with a closer look at its timeless storytelling and themes, understanding how it continues to resonate with audiences across generations.

At the heart of "It's a Wonderful Life" lies a narrative that transcends the constraints of its temporal setting. The story of George Bailey, portrayed by the incomparable Jimmy Stewart, unfolds with a poignant simplicity that belies its profound impact. As we traverse the decades and enter the fictional town of Bedford Falls, we are greeted not merely by characters on the screen but by archetypes that echo the universal struggles, dreams, and triumphs of the human experience.

The film's enduring appeal can be attributed, in part, to its ability to distill complex human emotions and existential dilemmas into a narrative that feels both intimate and expansive. George Bailey's journey from youthful aspirations to the brink of despair encapsulates the universal theme of the individual grappling with their place in the world. In this, the film becomes a mirror reflecting the aspirations and fears harbored by individuals across different eras.

Central to the film's timeless storytelling is its exploration of the ripple effect of one's life on the lives of others. The narrative device of Clarence, the endearing angel seeking his wings, allows us to witness not just the events of George Bailey's life but the immeasurable impact his choices have on those around him. This exploration of interconnectedness and the profound influence of seemingly small actions transcends the boundaries of time, speaking to the collective consciousness of humanity.

Moreover, "It's a Wonderful Life" doesn't shy away from the darker aspects of the human experience. George Bailey's struggles with financial ruin, dashed dreams, and existential despair are stark reminders of the challenges that accompany the pursuit of a meaningful life. The film doesn't paint an idyllic, sugar-coated portrait of existence but rather confronts the harsh realities with a sincerity that resonates with viewers facing their own trials and tribulations.

The film's central message—that each life has inherent value and meaning—remains a guiding light that pierces through the fog of doubt and despair. This theme is encapsulated in George Bailey's realization that his life, though filled with hardships and unfulfilled dreams, has woven a tapestry of love, sacrifice, and shared moments that define the very essence of a wonderful life. It's a message that transcends the temporal setting of post-war America and speaks to the universal human quest for purpose and fulfillment.

"It's a Wonderful Life" also stands as a testament to the power of redemption and second chances. The film portrays

George Bailey's transformative journey as he confronts his own disillusionment and contemplates a world without his presence. The alternate reality presented to him becomes a canvas upon which the film paints a vivid portrait of the positive influence one person can have on the lives of others. This theme of redemption, of finding hope and purpose even in the darkest moments, resonates with audiences as a timeless beacon of inspiration.

The film's enduring relevance is further underscored by its exploration of the tension between individual dreams and communal responsibilities. George Bailey's internal conflict, torn between personal aspirations and familial duties, is a narrative thread that weaves through the fabric of human experience. In an era marked by rapid societal changes and shifting values, this theme continues to strike a chord with viewers navigating the delicate balance between personal ambition and the interconnected web of relationships.

Additionally, the film's portrayal of the antagonist, the wealthy and heartless Mr. Potter, introduces a timeless commentary on the moral complexities of power and wealth. Mr. Potter becomes a symbol of unchecked capitalism and the potential consequences of prioritizing personal gain over the well-being of the community. This theme resonates not only with the post-war audience but continues to echo in discussions about societal inequality and the ethical responsibilities of those in positions of influence.

As we reflect on the timeless storytelling and themes of "It's a Wonderful Life," we find ourselves immersed in a narrative that transcends the boundaries of its release date. The film's ability to encapsulate the complexities of the human condition, its exploration of interconnectedness and redemption, and its poignant commentary on individual and communal values ensure that its resonance endures, inviting each generation to rediscover the magic within its frames.

In the chapters that follow, we will delve deeper into the impact of "It's a Wonderful Life" on pop culture, its technical filmmaking achievements, and the critical reception and analysis that have solidified its place as a Christmas Eve classic for the ages. But as we continue this journey, let us carry with us the timeless lessons and storytelling brilliance that define the very essence of this cinematic masterpiece—a film that invites us to ponder our own wonderful lives and the profound impact we have on the world around us.

In the hallowed halls of Christmas cinema, few films have left as indelible a mark as Frank Capra's "It's a Wonderful Life." Beyond its enchanting storytelling and timeless themes, this cinematic gem has carved a permanent place in the annals of pop culture. As we explore the impact it has had on the collective consciousness, we witness how George Bailey's journey has become more than a tale of one man's redemption—it has become a cultural touchstone, influencing everything from television to advertising and even language itself.

Television Broadcast Tradition:

"It's a Wonderful Life" may have been released in 1946, but its ascent to iconic status can be attributed in part to a seemingly serendipitous turn of events in the 1970s. Due to a lapse in copyright protection, the film found itself in the public domain, leading to its widespread and almost incessant broadcast on television during the holiday season. This unintentional generosity from the film's rights holders unwittingly transformed it into an annual ritual for families across the United States.

Generations of viewers found solace and inspiration in George Bailey's journey, tuning in each year to witness the heartwarming tale unfold. The film's annual television broadcasts became a cultural phenomenon, solidifying its place as a Christmas tradition. Families would gather around their television sets, eagerly awaiting the familiar sights and sounds of Bedford Falls, creating an enduring connection between the film and the holiday season.

Language and References:

"It's a Wonderful Life" didn't just enter the homes of millions through television screens; it permeated the very language we use. Phrases like "It's a wonderful life" and "Every time a bell rings, an angel gets his wings" have become ingrained in popular lexicon, transcending the boundaries of the film itself. These lines, uttered by characters in moments of joy and revelation, have taken on a life of their own, invoked in conversations, greeting cards, and even in the annual retelling of the film's narrative.

Beyond direct quotes, the film's thematic elements have seeped into cultural discourse. The idea of evaluating one's life and recognizing the profound impact of small acts of kindness has become a recurring theme in discussions about personal growth and communal responsibility. George Bailey's journey serves as a template for introspection, inspiring individuals to reflect on their own lives and consider the interconnectedness of their actions.

Parodies and Homages:

A testament to its cultural ubiquity, "It's a Wonderful Life" has been the subject of countless parodies and homages across various media. Television shows, animated series, and films have paid tribute to the iconic scenes and characters of Capra's masterpiece. The film's influence extends beyond the holiday genre, with creators across genres finding inspiration in its storytelling and themes.

One notable example is the animated series "The Simpsons," which dedicated an entire episode, titled "It's a Mad, Mad, Mad, Mad Marge," to a parody of the iconic film. The Simpsons' unique brand of humor provided a fresh lens through which to view the familiar narrative, showcasing the enduring appeal of "It's a Wonderful Life" across different cultural contexts.

Advertising and Commercialization:

The film's impact on pop culture extends into the realm of advertising and commercialization, where its themes are leveraged to evoke a sense of nostalgia and emotional resonance. Advertisements during the holiday season often tap into the familiar tropes established by "It's a Wonderful Life"—from small-town charm to the redemptive power of community.

Moreover, the characters themselves have become recognizable figures in the marketing landscape. Images of George Bailey, Clarence the angel, and the idyllic Bedford Falls are frequently employed to evoke a sense of warmth and familiarity, creating an emotional connection with consumers. The commercialization of the film not only reinforces its status as a cultural touchstone but also ensures its enduring presence in the contemporary holiday zeitgeist.

Influence on Filmmaking:

Beyond its direct impact on popular culture, "It's a Wonderful Life" has influenced subsequent generations of filmmakers. Its narrative structure, characterized by a retrospective examination of a character's life, has become a template for films exploring themes of redemption and self-discovery. The film's ability to blend heartfelt emotion with social commentary has inspired directors seeking to create works that resonate on both personal and societal levels.

The enduring legacy of "It's a Wonderful Life" is evident in the numerous films that have drawn inspiration from its narrative, characters, and themes. From small-town dramas to modern retellings of the redemption story, the influence of Capra's masterpiece can be discerned in the fabric of contemporary filmmaking.

Fan Celebrations and Events:

As with any cultural phenomenon, "It's a Wonderful Life" has spawned a community of devoted fans who celebrate the film in various ways. Festivals, screenings, and themed events dedicated to the movie have become annual traditions for enthusiasts seeking to share the joy of George Bailey's journey with like-minded individuals. These gatherings not only reinforce the film's cultural significance but also create a sense of community among fans who find solace and inspiration in its enduring message.

In conclusion, the impact of "It's a Wonderful Life" on pop culture is a testament to the enduring power of storytelling. From its humble beginnings as a holiday release in post-war America to its status as a perennial television favorite, the film has become woven into the fabric of the Christmas season. Its influence extends far beyond the confines of the screen, shaping the way we speak, the stories we tell, and the values we hold dear. As we continue our exploration of this cinematic treasure, we do so with an awareness of the profound and lasting impact it has had on the cultural landscape.

Technical Filmmaking Achievements

In the timeless landscape of Christmas cinema, "It's a Wonderful Life" stands as a beacon of cinematic brilliance, a testament to the artistry of Frank Capra and his creative collaborators. Beyond its heartwarming narrative and universal themes, the film is distinguished by its technical filmmaking achievements. As we delve into the intricacies of its production, we uncover the innovative techniques and artistic choices that have contributed to its enduring legacy.

Innovative Use of Special Effects:

"It's a Wonderful Life" was crafted in an era where special effects were in their infancy compared to contemporary standards, yet the film showcased a pioneering spirit in their application. One standout sequence is George Bailey's journey through an alternate reality, a fantastical landscape crafted with inventive visual effects for its time. The use of miniatures, matte paintings, and rear-projection techniques seamlessly blended to create a dreamlike world that remains a cinematic marvel.

In the scene where George experiences a world without his existence, the transformation of Bedford Falls into the bleak Pottersville showcases Capra's commitment to achieving visual impact through practical effects. The alteration of familiar locations, achieved through changes in lighting, set design, and atmospheric conditions, demonstrated a meticulous attention to detail that elevated the film's visual storytelling.

Innovative Cinematography and Lighting:

Cinematographer Joseph Walker collaborated closely with Capra to bring "It's a Wonderful Life" to life visually. The film showcases innovative camera work and lighting techniques that contributed to its distinct aesthetic. The chiaroscuro lighting in key scenes, such as George's confrontation with Mr. Potter, not only emphasized the emotional intensity but also added a noir-esque quality to the film, heightening the contrast between good and evil.

The film's intimate moments are captured with a delicate touch, utilizing soft lighting and warm tones to evoke a sense of nostalgia and comfort. This approach is particularly evident in scenes within the Bailey household, emphasizing the warmth and love that permeates George's home. Such thoughtful cinematography enhances the emotional resonance of the narrative, inviting viewers to connect more deeply with the characters and their struggles.

Art Direction and Set Design:

The art direction and set design of "It's a Wonderful Life" play a pivotal role in transporting audiences to the charming small town of Bedford Falls. Capra, known for his meticulous attention to detail, collaborated with art director Jack Okey to create an authentic and immersive environment. The set, while limited by budget constraints, exudes a sense of coziness and familiarity, becoming a character in its own right.

The transformation of the set to depict the contrasting realities of Bedford Falls and Pottersville required precision and ingenuity. The use of practical effects, such as changing signage and atmospheric alterations, showcased the resourcefulness of the filmmaking team. The attention to period-specific details in set design contributed to the film's ability to evoke a nostalgic longing for a bygone era.

Innovative Sound Design and Music:

The sound design and musical score of "It's a Wonderful Life" contribute significantly to its emotional impact. Composer Dimitri Tiomkin's evocative score enhances the film's emotional beats, underscoring moments of joy, despair, and redemption. The iconic use of holiday songs and hymns, woven seamlessly into the narrative, elevates the festive atmosphere and adds to the film's enduring appeal.

Sound designer Clem Portman played a crucial role in capturing the ambient sounds of Bedford Falls, further immersing audiences in the film's world. From the bustling streets to the angelic chime signaling an angel getting its wings, the sound design enhances the film's emotional beats and contributes to its immersive quality. The film's commitment to audio excellence, considering the technological limitations of its time, is a testament to the dedication of its creative team.

Groundbreaking Editing Techniques:

The editing of "It's a Wonderful Life," helmed by William Hornbeck, is a masterclass in narrative pacing and emotional storytelling. The film employs innovative editing techniques to seamlessly weave together George Bailey's past, present, and alternate reality. The use of cross-cutting during the pivotal building and loan crisis scenes, juxtaposing the frantic search for misplaced money with the Christmas festivities at home, adds a layer of tension and urgency to the narrative.

The editing also plays a crucial role in the film's emotional climax. As George races through Bedford Falls, desperately seeking validation for his existence, the rapid montage of scenes from his life punctuates the emotional crescendo. This editing technique not only conveys the overwhelming emotional turmoil within George but also allows viewers to experience the impact of his actions on the community.

Performance and Direction:

While not a technical aspect in the traditional sense, the performances directed by Frank Capra are integral to the film's technical brilliance. Capra's ability to elicit authentic and nuanced performances from his cast, particularly James Stewart as George Bailey, is a testament to his directorial prowess. Stewart's portrayal of a man grappling with the complexities of life, love, and despair anchors the film emotionally, ensuring its resonance with audiences.

Capra's directorial choices, including his use of deep focus to capture foreground and background action in a single frame, contribute to the film's immersive quality. The fluidity of the camera, coupled with precise blocking of actors, creates a visual language that enhances the storytelling. Capra's directorial vision, coupled with the technical expertise of his team, elevates "It's a Wonderful Life" beyond a simple holiday tale, turning it into a cinematic experience that continues to captivate audiences.

In conclusion, the technical filmmaking achievements of "It's a Wonderful Life" showcase the innovative spirit of its creators. From groundbreaking visual effects to evocative cinematography, meticulous art direction to immersive sound design, the film stands as a testament to the collaborative effort of a dedicated creative team. As we continue our exploration of this cinematic masterpiece, let us do so with an appreciation for the technical brilliance that has contributed to its enduring legacy.

In the pantheon of Christmas cinema, "It's a Wonderful Life" stands as a beacon of heartfelt storytelling and enduring warmth. Beyond the realm of its narrative and technical achievements, the film's critical reception and subsequent analyses have added layers of understanding to its timeless appeal. As we venture into the realm of critical assessments, we explore how initial receptions shaped the film's trajectory and how later analyses have deepened our appreciation for this cinematic masterpiece.

Critical Reception:

Upon its release in 1946, "It's a Wonderful Life" faced a mixed critical reception. Despite boasting the talents of director Frank Capra and actor James Stewart, the film struggled to make a significant impact at the box office. The post-war audience, perhaps yearning for more lighthearted fare, found the film's exploration of existential dilemmas and the darker aspects of life less appealing during a period of optimism.

Some critics of the time noted the film's sentimental tone, with accusations of Capra indulging in idealized portrayals of small-town America. The narrative's exploration of George Bailey's struggles and the consequences of his choices, while resonant for some, was perceived by others as overly moralistic. The film's initial lukewarm reception failed to reflect the profound impact it would later have on audiences and the cultural zeitgeist.

It wasn't until subsequent years, particularly with the advent of television broadcasts, that "It's a Wonderful Life" found its rightful place in the hearts of viewers. The annual holiday airings allowed audiences to rediscover the film, and its themes of redemption, community, and the enduring value of an individual life struck a chord that resonated far beyond its initial release.

Modern Reappraisal and Academic Analysis:

As time unfolded, "It's a Wonderful Life" underwent a remarkable transformation in critical perception. Modern reappraisals of the film have recognized its depth, complexity, and enduring relevance, leading to its inclusion in discussions of American cinema and cultural heritage.

Exploration of Existential Themes:

One facet that contemporary analyses often delve into is the film's exploration of existential themes. The character of George Bailey serves as a lens through which the audience contemplates the meaning of life, the impact of one's choices, and the interconnectedness of individual lives. The film's narrative structure, moving from George's contemplation of suicide to a reflective examination of his life, invites viewers to engage with profound philosophical questions.

The crisis faced by George Bailey, a man who feels shackled by responsibilities and unfulfilled dreams, resonates with the human experience. Modern analyses appreciate how the film navigates the complexities of identity, purpose, and the pursuit of happiness. George's journey becomes a universal allegory for individuals grappling with the existential quandaries that accompany the human condition.

Capraesque Optimism vs. Dark Realities:

Frank Capra's signature optimism, often referred to as "Capraesque," is a central element of "It's a Wonderful Life." However, modern analyses have explored the nuanced interplay between Capra's idealism and the film's darker undercurrents. While the film ultimately champions the triumph of goodness and community, it does not shy away from portraying the harsh realities of life.

The character of Mr. Potter, the embodiment of greed and callous capitalism, serves as a stark contrast to the altruistic values championed by George Bailey. Modern critics appreciate how the film acknowledges the existence of malevolence in the world, questioning the viability of an idyllic Bedford Falls in the face of unscrupulous figures like Potter. This juxtaposition adds layers to the film's social commentary, prompting viewers to confront the dualities inherent in society.

Feminist and Gender Perspectives:

As critical perspectives evolved, feminist analyses of "It's a Wonderful Life" began to emerge. The film's portrayal of Mary Bailey, initially seen as a devoted wife and mother, has been revisited through a feminist lens. Critics acknowledge the constraints of the era in which the film was made but also highlight Mary's agency and resilience.

Mary's role in supporting George during times of adversity and her agency in shaping their family's destiny have been recognized as essential components of the film's narrative. While the film adheres to certain gender norms of its time, feminist interpretations celebrate Mary's strength as a character who, in her own way, contributes to the film's exploration of familial and societal values.

Impact on Popular Culture as a Critical Indicator:

One of the most telling signs of a film's enduring significance is its impact on popular culture. "It's a Wonderful Life" has not only become a beloved holiday tradition but also a cultural touchstone referenced across various media. Its enduring popularity, evidenced by annual television broadcasts, parodies, and homages, speaks to its resonance with audiences over the decades.

Contemporary critics often use the film's cultural impact as a critical indicator of its enduring value. The fact that it has become synonymous with the holiday season and continues to capture the hearts of new generations attests to its ability to transcend temporal and cultural boundaries.

Legacy and Awards Recognition:

While the film did not receive widespread awards recognition upon its release, its legacy has been acknowledged in subsequent years. James Stewart's performance as George Bailey has been celebrated as one of the actor's finest, and the American Film Institute has included "It's a Wonderful Life" in various lists, cementing its status as a classic.

In 1990, the film was selected for preservation in the United States National Film Registry by the Library of Congress, recognizing its cultural, historical, and aesthetic significance. This official acknowledgment underscores the film's enduring impact on American cinema and its importance in the broader cultural landscape.

Conclusion:

In the realm of critical reception and analysis, "It's a Wonderful Life" has experienced a journey as profound as its protagonist, George Bailey. From a modestly received post-war release to a perennial holiday favorite, the film has weathered the ebb and flow of critical perspectives, emerging as a timeless classic cherished by audiences worldwide.

Modern analyses appreciate the film's thematic depth, its exploration of existential quandaries, and the delicate balance between Capra's optimism and the darker realities of life. The feminist reevaluation of Mary Bailey's character adds a contemporary lens to the film's portrayal of gender roles, while its impact on popular culture stands as a testament to its enduring relevance.

As we continue our exploration of "It's a Wonderful Life," let us navigate the terrain of critical reception and analysis with an awareness of the rich tapestry of insights woven by critics, scholars, and audiences alike. In doing so, we honor the film's journey from initial reception to cultural cornerstone, recognizing its place in the annals of cinematic history.

Chapter 2 - Home Alone (1990)
Memorable Slapstick Comedy

In the delightful realm of holiday cinema, few films capture the spirit of mischief and merriment as effectively as "Home Alone." Released in 1990 and directed by Chris Columbus, this family comedy has etched itself into the collective memory with its heartwarming narrative and, notably, its unforgettable slapstick comedy. As we explore the enduring charm of Kevin McCallister's misadventures, we'll unravel the artistry behind the film's slapstick elements and how they contribute to its timeless appeal.

Physical Comedy Mastery:

"Home Alone" unfolds as a symphony of physical comedy, with young Kevin McCallister (played by Macaulay Culkin) at the center of this comedic orchestration. The film's premise—Kevin accidentally left behind while his family embarks on a holiday trip—sets the stage for a series of slapstick gags that range from cleverly choreographed to downright chaotic.

Central to the film's success in this realm is Culkin's natural talent for physical comedy. His expressive face, impeccable timing, and fearless commitment to the pratfalls and stunts elevate Kevin's antics beyond mere slapstick into a form of comedic ballet. From the iconic aftershave scene to the perfectly executed paint cans to the face, Culkin's comedic prowess transforms Kevin's predicament into a source of endless laughter.

Ingenious Booby Traps:

A hallmark of "Home Alone" is Kevin's ingenious use of booby traps to thwart the bumbling burglars, Harry and Marv (played by Joe Pesci and Daniel Stern). The slapstick brilliance lies not only in the elaborate traps themselves but also in the meticulous setup and execution. Each trap is a meticulously crafted punchline to a comedic setup, and the escalating absurdity of the situations enhances the comedic impact.

The traps are a fusion of classic slapstick elements—physical harm delivered in a humorous manner—and ingenious, Rube Goldberg-inspired contraptions. From flying paint cans to scalding doorknobs, the film takes inspiration from classic slapstick while infusing it with a creative, holiday-themed twist. The meticulous planning and execution of these traps contribute to the film's enduring status as a slapstick comedy classic.

Painful Humor and Resilience:

At the heart of slapstick comedy lies the tension between pain and humor, and "Home Alone" navigates this balance with finesse. Kevin's encounters with the burglars result in a series of slapstick injuries, from Marv's tarantula-induced scream to Harry's numerous head injuries. The exaggerated reactions, coupled with the over-the-top sound effects, amplify the comedic impact of these moments.

What sets "Home Alone" apart is Kevin's resilience in the face of adversity. While the burglars suffer comical injuries, Kevin himself endures his fair share of physical challenges. Yet, his ability to outsmart the burglars and turn the tables transforms these moments of potential pain into sources of triumph and humor. This resilience adds depth to the film's slapstick comedy, emphasizing that Kevin is not merely a victim but an active participant in the comedic chaos.

Cinematic Influences and Homages:

Chris Columbus, the director of "Home Alone," drew inspiration from classic slapstick comedies of the past while infusing the film with his own directorial flair. The influence of directors like Buster Keaton and Charlie Chaplin, pioneers of silent-era slapstick, is evident in the film's physical comedy sequences. The emphasis on visual gags, pratfalls, and expressive reactions pays homage to the timeless appeal of these comedic masters.

Additionally, the film incorporates a nod to the golden age of slapstick through its inclusion of the fictional gangster film "Angels with Filthy Souls." The scenes featuring Johnny, the gun-wielding gangster, provide a clever homage to the gritty crime films of the 1930s and 1940s, adding a meta layer to the film's comedic tapestry. These nods to cinematic history enrich the slapstick elements with a sense of homage and celebration of the genre's enduring legacy.

Timing and Pacing:

The success of slapstick comedy often hinges on impeccable timing and pacing, and "Home Alone" excels in this regard. The film's comedic beats are expertly orchestrated, with moments of tension building to crescendos of laughter. Whether it's the burglars falling victim to Kevin's traps or Kevin navigating the challenges of being home alone, the film's pacing ensures that the audience is consistently engaged and entertained.

The strategic use of silence in certain comedic sequences, reminiscent of silent film conventions, allows the physical comedy to take center stage. Culkin's expressive face and body language become key components in delivering punchlines without the need for extensive dialogue. This reliance on visual storytelling and well-timed physical comedy contributes to the film's universal appeal, transcending language barriers and resonating with audiences of all ages.

Childhood Fantasy and Empowerment:

At its core, "Home Alone" taps into a universal childhood fantasy of outsmarting adults and reveling in newfound independence. Kevin's ability to outwit the burglars and navigate the challenges of being alone at home resonates with viewers of all ages, as it captures the spirit of childhood imagination and resourcefulness.

The film provides a sense of empowerment for its young protagonist, and this empowerment is amplified through the lens of slapstick comedy. Kevin's ability to turn the tables on the bumbling burglars transforms the potential threat into a source of comedic comeuppance. In this way, slapstick becomes a tool for storytelling, emphasizing Kevin's resilience and ingenuity in the face of adversity.

Heartwarming Comedy:

Beyond the physical antics and comedic chaos, "Home Alone" infuses its slapstick elements with a heartwarming quality. The film balances its comedic setpieces with moments of genuine emotion, particularly in Kevin's interactions with his neighbor, Old Man Marley, and his eventual reconciliation with his family.

This blend of humor and heart is a hallmark of Chris Columbus's directorial style, and it elevates "Home Alone" beyond a mere slapstick comedy to a film with enduring emotional resonance. The laughter induced by Kevin's slapstick escapades is complemented by moments of reflection, adding depth to the film's narrative and reinforcing its status as a beloved holiday classic.

Legacy and Continued Appeal:

As the years have passed, "Home Alone" has not only retained its status as a cherished holiday classic but has also solidified its place in the pantheon of slapstick comedy. The film's legacy is evident in its continued popularity, with new generations of viewers discovering and embracing its timeless humor.

The enduring appeal of "Home Alone" lies in its ability to evoke laughter through physical comedy while also capturing the essence of childhood wonder and resilience. The film's slapstick elements, from ingenious booby traps to exaggerated pratfalls, contribute to its status as a cinematic gem that transcends generational boundaries.

Conclusion:

In the realm of holiday cinema, "Home Alone" stands as a testament to the enduring magic of slapstick comedy. Through the mischievous adventures of Kevin McCallister and the hapless burglars, the film weaves a tapestry of physical comedy mastery, ingenious booby traps, and a perfect balance of pain and humor. Drawing inspiration from cinematic influences, incorporating childhood fantasies, and infusing heartwarming moments, "Home Alone" has carved a permanent place in the hearts of audiences worldwide.

As we revel in the laughter induced by Kevin's slapstick escapades, we do so with an appreciation for the artistry behind the film's comedic brilliance. "Home Alone" not only showcases the enduring appeal of slapstick but also exemplifies the power of humor to transcend time, bringing joy to viewers of all ages during the holiday season and beyond.

Darker Elements and Violence

In the festive landscape of holiday cinema, "Home Alone" unfolds as a delightful family comedy, a timeless tale of youthful ingenuity and the triumph of resourcefulness. Yet, beneath the veneer of holiday cheer and slapstick antics, the film reveals a nuanced interplay of darker elements and violence. As we delve into this aspect of "Home Alone," we explore how the film navigates the fine line between comedic chaos and moments of genuine peril, adding layers of complexity to its narrative and contributing to its enduring intrigue.

The Premise and the Absent Family:

At its core, "Home Alone" introduces a premise that, while whimsical in its execution, carries an underlying sense of darkness. The accidental abandonment of eight-year-old Kevin McCallister by his family as they embark on a holiday trip sets the stage for the film's narrative. The notion of a child being left behind, unnoticed in the bustling preparations for a family vacation, taps into a primal fear and vulnerability.

The darker undertones emerge as Kevin grapples with the reality of his solitude. The vast, empty McCallister residence, initially a playground for Kevin's mischief, becomes a symbol of isolation. The film, through visual storytelling and subtle cues, communicates the emotional weight of Kevin's predicament, creating a sense of unease that lingers beneath the comedic surface.

Old Man Marley and Misconceptions:

As the narrative unfolds, the character of Old Man Marley, the mysterious neighbor rumored to be a serial killer, introduces an additional layer of darkness. The neighborhood's urban legends surrounding Marley contribute to a sense of foreboding, heightening the film's tension. The film plays with the audience's expectations, leading them to anticipate a sinister revelation regarding Marley's true nature.

The eventual revelation, however, subverts these expectations. Marley's character arc becomes a poignant exploration of loneliness, familial estrangement, and the impact of misconceptions. The film deftly navigates the fine line between dark rumors and genuine human connection, using Old Man Marley as a vessel to challenge preconceived notions and offer a message of empathy.

The Burglars: Harry and Marv:

The introduction of the bumbling burglars, Harry and Marv, injects an element of violence into the film's comedic narrative. The duo's relentless pursuit of breaking into the McCallister residence becomes a source of peril for Kevin and a catalyst for the film's physical comedy. While the violence inflicted upon Harry and Marv is exaggerated and presented in a slapstick manner, the threat they pose introduces an element of danger.

The escalation of violence, portrayed through Kevin's ingenious booby traps, transforms the film into a chaotic battleground. From scalding doorknobs to tarantulas, each trap carries the potential for harm, albeit in a cartoonish and exaggerated fashion. The juxtaposition of violence with humor blurs the lines between peril and comedy, creating a unique tonal balance that defines "Home Alone."

Slapstick Violence and Comic Resilience:

"Home Alone" relies heavily on slapstick violence, a comedic tradition that dates back to classic silent cinema. The physical harm inflicted upon Harry and Marv, while exaggerated and unrealistic, draws inspiration from the traditions of physical comedy. The burglars become unwitting recipients of Kevin's inventive and often painful traps, leading to a series of pratfalls, collisions, and misfortunes.

The film's comedic resilience lies in the exaggerated reactions of Harry and Marv to the physical harm they endure. Instead of eliciting sympathy, the burglars' injuries become sources of humor. The cartoonish nature of the violence, coupled with the burglars' dogged determination to capture Kevin, transforms the potentially dark and menacing elements into a playground of chaotic hilarity.

Psychological Elements: Kevin's Fear and Empowerment:

Beyond the physical violence, "Home Alone" delves into psychological elements, particularly through Kevin's emotional journey. The initial fear and vulnerability experienced by the young protagonist as he navigates being alone contribute to the film's darker undertones. The use of shadows, eerie sounds, and suspenseful music heightens the sense of unease during Kevin's initial realization of his predicament.

However, as the narrative unfolds, Kevin's fear transforms into a sense of empowerment. His resourcefulness, clever planning, and ability to outsmart the burglars become symbols of resilience and independence. The film navigates the psychological terrain of a child facing adversity, utilizing both humor and moments of genuine emotional reflection to create a multidimensional character arc.

Balancing Dark Themes with Heartwarming Moments:

"Home Alone" expertly balances its darker elements with heartwarming moments that serve to alleviate tension and add depth to the narrative. Kevin's interactions with Old Man Marley, the film's emotional core, provide a counterbalance to the chaotic slapstick and potential peril. The revelation of Marley's true nature and the resolution of his estrangement from his family inject a dose of sentimentality into the film, creating a harmonious blend of tones.

The film's ultimate message of the importance of family, love, and understanding counteracts the potential darkness that lurks beneath the surface. Kevin's journey, from loneliness to empowerment, is mirrored in the emotional arcs of the supporting characters, offering a narrative resolution that transcends the chaotic events that unfold.

Legacy and Cultural Impact:

The juxtaposition of darker elements and violence within the comedic framework of "Home Alone" has contributed to its enduring cultural impact. The film's ability to navigate the fine line between peril and comedy, darkness and light, has resonated with audiences across generations. Its legacy is evident in its continued popularity as a holiday classic and a source of nostalgic joy.

"Home Alone" has become a cultural touchstone, referenced in various forms of media and embedded in the holiday traditions of millions. Its unique blend of slapstick violence, psychological elements, and heartwarming resolution has solidified its place as a film that transcends genre conventions, offering a nuanced and entertaining exploration of the complexities of childhood.

Conclusion:

As we explore the darker elements and violence within the comedic tapestry of "Home Alone," we recognize the film's ability to navigate a nuanced terrain. From the primal fear of abandonment to the slapstick violence inflicted upon the burglars, the film weaves a narrative that transcends simple genre categorizations. The balancing act between darkness and light, danger and comedy, contributes to the film's enduring intrigue and cultural resonance.

In the end, "Home Alone" invites audiences into a world where chaos and laughter coexist, where the threat of danger is transformed into a playground of comedic mayhem. As we revisit the McCallister residence during the holiday season, we do so with an appreciation for the film's ability to navigate the complexities of childhood, family, and the enduring spirit of resourcefulness and resilience.

Christmas Sentimentality

In the vast landscape of holiday cinema, "Home Alone" stands as a perennial favorite, a timeless classic that transcends generations. While celebrated for its slapstick comedy and darker elements, the film's enduring charm also lies in its ability to evoke Christmas sentimentality. As we delve into this aspect of "Home Alone," we explore how the film weaves a tapestry of heartwarming moments, festive aesthetics, and thematic richness, creating a cinematic experience that captures the essence of the holiday season.

Festive Aesthetics and Iconic Imagery:

"Home Alone" immerses viewers in a world adorned with the festive trappings of Christmas, creating an aesthetic tapestry that resonates with holiday sentimentality. The McCallister residence, decked with twinkling lights, festive decorations, and a towering Christmas tree, serves as a visual embodiment of yuletide cheer. The film embraces the idyllic imagery associated with Christmas, inviting audiences into a warm and inviting world.

The iconic scenes of Kevin wandering through a snow-covered neighborhood, adorned with charming Christmas lights, contribute to the film's visual appeal. The juxtaposition of winter landscapes with the glow of holiday decorations enhances the festive atmosphere, creating a cinematic tableau that reflects the magic of Christmas. The film's commitment to visual storytelling through festive aesthetics establishes an immediate connection with the viewer's sense of holiday sentimentality.

Soundtrack and Musical Identity:

The film's musical score, composed by John Williams, plays a pivotal role in amplifying its Christmas sentimentality. Williams, known for his ability to capture the emotional essence of a film through music, infuses "Home Alone" with a melodic and evocative soundtrack. The whimsical and heartwarming notes of "Somewhere in My Memory," the film's signature theme, become synonymous with the holiday season.

The soundtrack's integration of classic Christmas tunes, including "O Holy Night" and "Carol of the Bells," further contributes to the film's festive musical identity. The use of familiar holiday melodies serves as a nostalgic touchstone, evoking memories of Christmases past and enhancing the overall sentimentality of the film. The soundtrack becomes a companion to the visual elements, creating a multisensory experience that resonates with audiences on an emotional level.

Family Themes and Reconciliation:

At its core, "Home Alone" weaves a narrative thread centered around family themes, a core element of Christmas sentimentality. The accidental abandonment of Kevin by his family becomes a catalyst for reflection on the importance of familial bonds. The initial chaos and frustration give way to a deeper exploration of love, understanding, and reconciliation as the film unfolds.

Kevin's journey becomes a microcosm of the larger theme of family unity during the holiday season. The film acknowledges the imperfections and challenges within families but ultimately emphasizes the enduring strength of familial ties. The resolution, where the family reunites and embraces the true spirit of Christmas, resonates with viewers as a celebration of togetherness and forgiveness.

Emotional Resonance and Childhood Wonder:

"Home Alone" captures the essence of childhood wonder and the emotional resonance of Christmas through Kevin's eyes. The film taps into the magic of the season, portraying the excitement of a child waking up on Christmas morning to discover presents under the tree. Kevin's interactions with the festive elements around him, from decorating the tree to sled rides down the stairs, evoke a sense of innocent joy and wonder.

The film's portrayal of Christmas as a time of magic and possibility contributes to its sentimentality. Kevin's belief in Santa Claus, manifested through his encounter with Old Man Marley and the enigmatic neighbor's timely intervention, adds a layer of enchantment to the narrative. The film invites viewers to rediscover the magic of Christmas through the lens of childhood innocence, eliciting a nostalgic longing for the simplicity and wonder of youth.

Old Man Marley's Redemption:

Within the broader theme of Christmas sentimentality, the character arc of Old Man Marley emerges as a poignant exploration of redemption and the transformative power of the season. Initially presented as an ominous figure shrouded in neighborhood folklore, Marley's true nature is gradually revealed, adding a layer of emotional complexity to the narrative.

The resolution of Marley's estrangement from his family becomes a heartwarming subplot that aligns with the film's overarching themes of forgiveness and second chances. The emotional exchange between Marley and Kevin, underscored by the backdrop of Christmas Eve, resonates with viewers on a deep emotional level. Marley's redemption serves as a testament to the healing and transformative potential of the holiday season.

Comedic Heart and Warmth:

While "Home Alone" is celebrated for its comedic chaos, its heart and warmth contribute significantly to its Christmas sentimentality. The film balances slapstick humor with moments of genuine emotion, creating a narrative that elicits both laughter and tears. Kevin's resourcefulness, the burglars' bumbling antics, and the film's overall sense of playfulness contribute to its comedic heart.

The warmth emanates from the genuine connections formed within the narrative, from Kevin's bond with Old Man Marley to the family's reunion. The film acknowledges the challenges and imperfections within familial relationships but ultimately emphasizes the unconditional love that defines the holiday season. The comedic elements, infused with genuine emotion, create a narrative tapestry that resonates with the viewer's sense of Christmas sentimentality.

Cinematic Homage to Christmas Classics:

"Home Alone" pays homage to classic Christmas films, drawing inspiration from the sentimentality and thematic richness of holiday cinema. The film incorporates nods to cinematic traditions, including the fictional gangster film "Angels with Filthy Souls" and its sequel. These cinematic references add a meta layer to the narrative, inviting viewers to engage with the film within the context of Christmas movie traditions.

The incorporation of classic Christmas tunes, reminiscent of the golden age of Hollywood musicals, further enhances the film's homage to cinematic history. By weaving these references into its narrative, "Home Alone" becomes a cinematic heir to the legacy of Christmas classics, contributing to its status as a film that honors and perpetuates the sentimentality of the holiday genre.

Legacy and Continued Cultural Impact:

The enduring legacy of "Home Alone" as a holiday classic is intrinsically tied to its ability to evoke Christmas sentimentality. The film's continued cultural impact, evidenced by its annual presence in holiday programming and its status as a cherished tradition, speaks to its resonance with audiences. Its themes of family, love, and the magic of Christmas have solidified its place in the hearts of viewers across generations.

"Home Alone" transcends its status as a mere comedy; it becomes a vessel for the spirit of Christmas, a cinematic experience that captures the multifaceted emotions associated with the holiday season. As audiences revisit the film year after year, they are not only treated to a display of comedic brilliance but also invited to immerse themselves in the timeless sentimentality that defines the magic of Christmas.

Conclusion:

In the heartwarming tapestry of "Home Alone," Christmas sentimentality emerges as a central thread that weaves together the film's visual, musical, and thematic elements. From the festive aesthetics that adorn the McCallister residence to the evocative soundtrack that resonates with holiday melodies, the film creates a multisensory experience that captures the magic of Christmas.

The themes of family, childhood wonder, redemption, and the transformative power of the season contribute to the film's sentimentality. The emotional resonance of Old Man Marley's redemption, the comedic heart that balances chaos with warmth, and the cinematic homage to Christmas classics establish "Home Alone" as a film that transcends genre conventions, becoming a cherished tradition that embodies the true spirit of the holiday season.

In the annals of cinematic history, few films have achieved the enduring legacy and cultural resonance of "Home Alone." Beyond its initial success as a holiday blockbuster, the film has woven itself into the fabric of popular culture, becoming a cherished classic that transcends generations. As we explore the legacy of "Home Alone" with fans and critics alike, we unravel the factors that have contributed to its lasting impact, examining how the film's blend of humor, heart, and holiday magic has secured its place as a beloved cinematic gem.

Generational Connection:

One of the most remarkable aspects of "Home Alone's" legacy is its ability to establish a generational connection. Originally released in 1990, the film continues to captivate audiences of all ages, with each new generation discovering and embracing its timeless charm. For many, "Home Alone" is not just a film; it's a shared experience, a holiday tradition passed down from parents to children.

The film's universal themes of family, resilience, and the magic of Christmas create a timeless appeal that resonates with viewers across different stages of life. Families revisit the McCallister residence each holiday season, introducing younger members to the mischievous antics of Kevin McCallister and the comedic chaos that ensues. The film's ability to bridge generational gaps and evoke a sense of nostalgia has solidified its status as a staple in the holiday cinematic canon.

Nostalgia and Tradition:

Nostalgia plays a pivotal role in "Home Alone's" enduring popularity. For those who grew up with the film, it represents a cherished part of their own childhood holiday memories. The familiar sights and sounds of the film, from the McCallister house adorned with Christmas lights to the iconic musical score, evoke a sense of nostalgia that transports viewers back to the innocence and wonder of their youth.

As a result, watching "Home Alone" becomes more than a mere viewing experience; it becomes a tradition. Families and friends gather annually to relive the escapades of Kevin, laugh at the burglars' foiled attempts, and savor the heartwarming moments that define the film. The annual ritual of watching "Home Alone" transforms the film into a cultural touchstone, a shared tradition that fosters a sense of togetherness and continuity.

Quotable Lines and Cultural References:

"Home Alone" has permeated popular culture through its memorable and oft-quoted lines. From Kevin's iconic scream to Marv's exasperated "Harry!" to the timeless "Keep the change, ya filthy animal," the film's dialogue has become ingrained in the collective lexicon. Fans not only revisit the film for its narrative but also delight in reciting these memorable lines, contributing to its cultural impact.

The film's influence extends beyond the screen, with its references appearing in various forms of media. From television shows and commercials to memes and social media, "Home Alone" continues to be a source of inspiration and cultural reference points. The enduring popularity of these quotes speaks to the film's ability to leave an indelible mark on popular discourse, further solidifying its legacy.

Interactive Engagement:

The advent of social media and digital platforms has given rise to interactive engagement with films, and "Home Alone" has embraced this shift with enthusiasm. Fans actively participate in online discussions, sharing their favorite moments, creating memes, and engaging in debates about the film's nuances. The communal experience of discussing and celebrating "Home Alone" on digital platforms has amplified its cultural presence and fostered a sense of community among fans.

Fan-generated content, from nostalgic fan art to creative reinterpretations of iconic scenes, further contributes to the interactive engagement surrounding the film. The participatory nature of online fandom has allowed "Home Alone" to evolve beyond a passive viewing experience into a dynamic and ongoing conversation that spans digital spaces.

Merchandising and Collectibles:

The film's legacy extends beyond the screen through a plethora of merchandise and collectibles. "Home Alone" has inspired a range of products, from holiday-themed ornaments and apparel to board games and home décor. The McCallister house, with its distinctive red door and green shutters, has become an iconic image that adorns everything from Christmas sweaters to cookie jars.

Collectors avidly seek out "Home Alone" memorabilia, turning the film into a cultural phenomenon that extends into the realms of consumer products. The enduring popularity of these items reflects not only the film's status as a beloved classic but also its ability to inspire a sense of festive nostalgia that fans are eager to incorporate into their holiday traditions.

Legacy With Critics:

Cinematic Endurance:

From its initial release to the present day, "Home Alone" has defied critical expectations, showcasing a cinematic endurance that transcends typical holiday fare. While some critics initially dismissed the film as a lightweight comedy, its staying power and continued popularity have prompted critical reevaluation. The enduring appeal of "Home Alone" challenges traditional notions of critical assessment, highlighting the importance of considering a film's cultural impact and enduring resonance.

Critics who revisit "Home Alone" often acknowledge its effectiveness in achieving what it sets out to do: entertain and capture the spirit of the holiday season. The film's ability to maintain relevance and captivate audiences decades after its release speaks to its cinematic craftsmanship and its understanding of the emotional and cultural dimensions that define enduring classics.

Balancing Comedy and Heart:

One aspect that has garnered critical appreciation is the film's adept balancing of comedy and heart. While "Home Alone" is undeniably a comedy, its success lies in its ability to infuse genuine emotion and thematic depth into the narrative. Critics have noted the film's capacity to deliver laughs through slapstick antics while simultaneously exploring universal themes of family, resilience, and the transformative power of the holiday season.

The comedic elements, from Kevin's ingenious booby traps to the burglars' hapless attempts, are complemented by moments of heartfelt sincerity. The film's emotional core, particularly in Kevin's interactions with Old Man Marley and the family's reunion, elevates it beyond the realm of standard comedies. Critics recognize that the film's enduring legacy is not solely due to its comedic brilliance but also to its ability to resonate on an emotional level.

Influence on Subsequent Films:

"Home Alone's" influence on subsequent films, particularly within the holiday genre, has not gone unnoticed by critics. The film's success paved the way for a wave of family-friendly holiday comedies that sought to capture a similar blend of humor, heart, and festive charm. While not every film achieved the same level of cultural impact, "Home Alone" set a precedent for the enduring appeal of holiday-centric narratives.

Critics acknowledge the film's role in shaping the landscape of holiday cinema, influencing both thematic and tonal elements embraced by later releases. The film's legacy can be seen in the countless attempts to replicate its formula, with varying degrees of success. As a result, "Home Alone" is not only a classic in its own right but also a touchstone that has left an indelible mark on the genre it helped define.

Reevaluation and Critical Appreciation:

Over time, there has been a noticeable reevaluation and critical appreciation for "Home Alone." What might have been dismissed as a simple family comedy upon its release is now recognized for its cultural impact, enduring popularity, and thematic richness. Critics have revisited the film with fresh eyes, acknowledging its contribution to the holiday genre and its ability to resonate with diverse audiences.

The film's inclusion in discussions of holiday classics and retrospectives dedicated to its cultural significance reflects a broader acknowledgment of its place in cinematic history. Critics, too, have come to appreciate the film's unique alchemy of humor, heart, and holiday spirit, recognizing that its enduring legacy extends far beyond the realm of conventional critical assessments.

Impact on Filmmaking and Genre Blending:

"Home Alone" has had a lasting impact on filmmaking approaches and genre blending. The film demonstrated that a holiday-centric narrative could seamlessly combine elements of comedy, family drama, and festive charm. Its success prompted filmmakers to explore the potential of blending genres within the context of holiday storytelling, leading to a diversification of approaches in subsequent films.

Critics have noted the film's influence on the evolution of the holiday genre, with a recognition that holiday films can transcend traditional genre boundaries. The willingness to incorporate slapstick humor, heartfelt moments, and a thematic focus on family dynamics has become a hallmark of successful holiday films. "Home Alone" stands as a pioneer in this genre-blending approach, shaping the expectations and possibilities for holiday storytelling in cinema.

Legacy as a Cultural Phenomenon:

Critics acknowledge that "Home Alone" has transcended its status as a film to become a cultural phenomenon. Its legacy extends beyond the boundaries of critical assessments, encompassing a broader cultural impact that has shaped holiday traditions and popular discourse. The film's ability to resonate with both critics and audiences alike highlights its versatility and enduring relevance.

As a cultural phenomenon, "Home Alone" is not simply a product of its time but a timeless work that continues to leave an indelible mark on the collective consciousness. Critics recognize that its legacy is not confined to the realm of cinema but extends into the fabric of holiday celebrations, creating a lasting imprint on the cultural landscape.

Conclusion:

"Home Alone's" legacy with fans and critics is a testament to its enduring power as a cinematic masterpiece. For fans, the film represents more than a holiday classic; it's a cherished tradition, a source of laughter, and a timeless experience that resonates across generations. The film's ability to inspire nostalgia, generate interactive engagement, and permeate popular culture speaks to its lasting impact.

On the critical front, "Home Alone" has transcended initial assessments to garner appreciation for its thematic richness, genre-blending innovation, and cultural significance. The film's enduring popularity challenges conventional notions of critical success, showcasing that a film's legacy is often measured by its ability to capture the hearts of audiences and become a cultural touchstone.

As we delve into the legacy of "Home Alone," we recognize that its impact goes beyond the screen; it lives on in the hearts of those who revisit the McCallister residence each holiday season. The film's legacy is not just about what happens on Christmas Eve but how it continues to shape and enrich the holiday experiences of fans around the world.

Chapter 3 - A Christmas Carol (1951)
Adaptation Choices Analysis

In the realm of Christmas cinema, Charles Dickens's timeless novella, "A Christmas Carol," has been a source of inspiration for numerous adaptations. From the silent film era to modern interpretations, filmmakers have grappled with the challenge of bringing Ebenezer Scrooge's transformative journey to life on the screen. In this analysis of adaptation choices, we explore the various cinematic renditions of "A Christmas Carol," examining the creative decisions that filmmakers have made to capture the essence of Dickens's classic tale and deliver its enduring message of redemption, compassion, and the true spirit of Christmas.

Period and Setting:

One of the initial decisions in adapting "A Christmas Carol" lies in the period and setting of the narrative. Dickens's original work is set in Victorian London, a time of social and economic upheaval. Filmmakers have grappled with the decision of whether to retain the novella's historical setting or to transpose the story to a different time and place.

Many adaptations, particularly those faithful to the source material, retain the Victorian setting. This decision allows filmmakers to capture the distinct atmosphere of 19th-century London, with its gas-lit streets, cobblestone alleys, and Victorian architecture. The period setting not only provides a visual feast for audiences but also serves to underscore the social issues central to Dickens's narrative, such as poverty, inequality, and the struggle for redemption.

However, some adaptations opt for a more contemporary or stylized setting. By updating the time period, filmmakers can draw parallels between Scrooge's world and contemporary issues. This choice allows for a more immediate resonance with modern audiences, emphasizing the universality of Dickens's themes. Whether set in Victorian England or a contemporary metropolis, the adaptation's period and setting are crucial choices that shape the visual and thematic elements of the film.

Scrooge's Portrayal:

At the heart of "A Christmas Carol" is the iconic character of Ebenezer Scrooge, a miserly and cold-hearted old man who undergoes a profound transformation. The portrayal of Scrooge is a critical adaptation choice, as it defines the emotional arc of the narrative. Filmmakers grapple with the challenge of capturing both the severity of Scrooge's miserliness and the vulnerability beneath his stern exterior.

Some adaptations lean into a more traditional depiction of Scrooge as a stern and almost caricatured figure. This portrayal emphasizes the severity of his miserly ways, with a focus on his disdain for Christmas and his employees. The challenge lies in balancing the character's harshness with hints of humanity that make his eventual redemption believable and emotionally resonant.

Other adaptations opt for a more nuanced portrayal of Scrooge, delving deeper into the psychological complexities that drive his behavior. These films explore the traumas and experiences that shaped Scrooge into the miser he has become.

This choice adds layers to the character, inviting audiences to empathize with his journey of self-discovery and redemption.

Additionally, the casting of Scrooge is a crucial choice. Whether portrayed by a seasoned actor known for their gravitas or a performer capable of infusing the character with vulnerability, the actor's interpretation significantly influences the adaptation's emotional impact. Scrooge's portrayal serves as the linchpin of the narrative, and adaptation choices related to his character resonate throughout the entire film.

Ghostly Apparitions:

Central to the supernatural elements of "A Christmas Carol" are the three ghostly apparitions that visit Scrooge on Christmas Eve. The Ghosts of Christmas Past, Present, and Yet to Come serve as catalysts for Scrooge's transformation, guiding him through a journey of self-reflection and revelation. Filmmakers face the challenge of bringing these otherworldly characters to life while maintaining the thematic weight of their interactions with Scrooge.

Adaptations vary in their interpretation of the ghosts, with some adhering closely to Dickens's descriptions and others taking creative liberties. The Ghost of Christmas Past, often portrayed as a ethereal and glowing figure, may be represented as a benevolent guide or a more enigmatic force, depending on the director's vision.

The Ghost of Christmas Present, characterized by abundance and generosity, is a visual and thematic contrast to the austere Scrooge. Filmmakers must decide how to portray the spirit's joviality and warmth, emphasizing the joy of the season while delivering poignant messages about the consequences of selfishness and neglect.

The Ghost of Christmas Yet to Come, often depicted as a foreboding figure in a shrouded robe, presents a particular challenge. Filmmakers must balance the eerie and ominous nature of this apparition with the emotional weight of its revelations about Scrooge's potential future. Some adaptations emphasize the grim and unsettling aspects of the Ghost of Christmas Yet to Come, heightening the stakes for Scrooge's redemption.

Structural Choices:

Adapting a novella into a feature-length film requires careful consideration of structural choices. Filmmakers must decide how faithfully to follow Dickens's narrative structure and which elements to emphasize or condense. Some adaptations maintain a strict adherence to the novella's episodic structure, faithfully recreating each of Scrooge's encounters with the ghosts and the glimpses into his past, present, and future.

Other adaptations take a more interpretative approach, reordering or combining certain elements to create a more cohesive cinematic narrative. This choice allows for a more dynamic and streamlined storytelling experience, condensing the novella's episodic nature into a more fluid and engaging structure.

Additionally, some adaptations choose to expand on certain elements of the novella, delving deeper into Scrooge's backstory, exploring secondary characters, or introducing new subplots. These structural expansions can provide additional context and emotional depth to the narrative, offering a fresh perspective on Dickens's classic tale.

Visual Style and Aesthetic Choices:

The visual style and aesthetic choices of an adaptation play a crucial role in shaping its cinematic identity. Filmmakers must decide on the overall look and feel of the film, considering factors such as cinematography, production design, and costume choices. These aesthetic decisions contribute to the film's atmosphere and its ability to immerse audiences in the world of "A Christmas Carol."

For adaptations set in Victorian London, the visual style often leans towards a rich and immersive period aesthetic. Cinematographers may use warm, candlelit tones to evoke the gas-lit streets of Dickensian London, and production designers meticulously recreate the architecture and fashion of the era. These choices transport audiences to a bygone time, enhancing the film's historical authenticity.

In contrast, adaptations with a contemporary or stylized setting may employ a more diverse visual palette. Filmmakers can experiment with lighting, color schemes, and camera techniques to convey the emotional tones of the narrative. The Ghosts' sequences, in particular, provide opportunities for creative and fantastical visuals, from the ethereal glow of the Ghost of Christmas Past to the festive abundance of the Ghost of Christmas Present.

Costume design also plays a pivotal role in conveying character and period authenticity. Scrooge's distinct attire, from his threadbare nightshirt to his tailored Victorian clothing, reflects his socioeconomic status and journey of redemption. The costumes of secondary characters, such as Bob Cratchit and Tiny Tim, contribute to the film's visual storytelling, emphasizing the stark contrasts in wealth and privilege.

Musical Score and Sound Design:

The musical score and sound design of an adaptation are essential elements that contribute to its emotional impact. Filmmakers must decide how to use music to underscore key moments, evoke the atmosphere of the narrative, and enhance the overall cinematic experience. The choice of musical themes, instruments, and soundscapes can elevate the film's emotional resonance and immerse audiences in the world of "A Christmas Carol."

Many adaptations feature a score that incorporates traditional Christmas carols, enhancing the festive atmosphere of the narrative. The use of familiar tunes, from "God Rest Ye Merry, Gentlemen" to "Hark! The Herald Angels Sing," establishes a connection with the holiday season and reinforces the film's thematic focus on Christmas spirit and goodwill.

Original compositions also play a crucial role in shaping the film's musical identity. Composers must create themes that capture the emotional nuances of Scrooge's journey, from the haunting melodies associated with the Ghosts to the triumphant crescendo accompanying his redemption. The musical score serves as a narrative companion, heightening the emotional beats and guiding audiences through the highs and lows of the story.

In terms of sound design, the adaptation choices extend to the use of ambient sounds, atmospheric effects, and dialogue delivery. The clinking of chains, the bustling streets of London, and the sounds of festive celebrations contribute to the immersive experience. Dialogue delivery, whether delivered with Dickensian eloquence or a more contemporary approach, influences the film's tone and accessibility to modern audiences.

Interpretation of Themes:

At the core of "A Christmas Carol" are timeless themes that explore the human condition, compassion, and the potential for personal redemption. Filmmakers face the challenge of interpreting these themes in a way that resonates with audiences while staying true to Dickens's vision. The adaptation choices related to thematic interpretation shape the film's narrative focus and emotional impact.

Central to the novella is the theme of redemption, and filmmakers must decide how to convey Scrooge's transformation convincingly. Some adaptations emphasize the gradual nature of his change, allowing audiences to witness the incremental shifts in his attitude and behavior. Others may opt for a more pronounced and dramatic transformation, punctuated by a climactic revelation of Scrooge's newfound generosity and empathy.

The theme of compassion and social responsibility is also integral to "A Christmas Carol." Filmmakers must decide how to portray Scrooge's awakening to the plight of the less fortunate, particularly through his interactions with the Cratchit family and Tiny Tim. The adaptation choices related to these moments influence the film's emphasis on social justice and the broader societal implications of Scrooge's redemption.

Additionally, the thematic exploration of time and its impact on human existence requires careful consideration. The Ghost of Christmas Yet to Come, representing the inexorable march of time, prompts Scrooge to confront his own mortality and the legacy he leaves behind. Filmmakers must decide how to convey this existential theme, whether through atmospheric visuals, symbolic imagery, or poignant dialogue.

Balancing Tradition and Innovation:

Ultimately, filmmakers face the delicate task of balancing tradition and innovation in their adaptation choices. While Dickens's novella provides a revered foundation, each adaptation offers an opportunity for creative expression and reinterpretation. Filmmakers must navigate the tension between staying true to the source material and introducing fresh perspectives that resonate with contemporary audiences.

Adaptations that hew closely to Dickens's original text may be celebrated for their fidelity to the classic tale. These films prioritize preserving the language, characters, and narrative structure of the novella, offering a cinematic experience that feels like a faithful retelling of the beloved story. The challenge lies in infusing freshness into a story that has been adapted countless times while honoring the timeless qualities that make "A Christmas Carol" enduring.

Conversely, adaptations that take liberties with the source material may be praised for their innovation and reinterpretation. These films may explore new facets of characters, introduce subplots, or reimagine the visual and thematic elements of the story. The challenge here is striking a balance between innovation and the preservation of the core elements that define "A Christmas Carol."

In conclusion, the adaptation choices in bringing "A Christmas Carol" to the screen are multifaceted and nuanced. From period and setting decisions to character portrayals, filmmakers navigate a complex landscape to capture the essence of Dickens's classic tale. Each adaptation becomes a cinematic journey through time, exploring the enduring themes of redemption, compassion, and the transformative power of the Christmas spirit.

Portrayals of Ebenezer Scrooge

At the heart of Charles Dickens's "A Christmas Carol" is the iconic character of Ebenezer Scrooge, a miserly and cold-hearted old man whose transformative journey forms the narrative's emotional core. The multifaceted nature of Scrooge's character allows for diverse interpretations in cinematic adaptations, offering actors the opportunity to delve into the complexities of a man wrestling with his past, present, and future. In this exploration of Ebenezer Scrooge's portrayals in various film adaptations, we delve into the nuanced performances that have brought this quintessential literary character to life on the screen.

Traditional Sternness:

Many adaptations choose to portray Scrooge in alignment with Dickens's original vision—a stern, severe, and almost caricatured figure consumed by his greed and disdain for all things festive. This traditional depiction often emphasizes Scrooge's miserliness through physical attributes such as his hunched posture, tightly pursed lips, and a perpetual scowl etched onto his face. These adaptations lean into the outward manifestations of Scrooge's miserly nature, creating a character whose very presence evokes a sense of foreboding.

In these portrayals, Scrooge's disdain for Christmas is palpable, his grumbling about the holiday and contemptuous dismissal of goodwill evident in every interaction. The emphasis on Scrooge as a caricature of miserliness serves a dual purpose—it establishes him as a clear antagonist while also laying the groundwork for a more dramatic and visually impactful transformation as the narrative unfolds.

Actors embodying this traditional sternness bring a theatricality to the role, using exaggerated facial expressions, sharp intonations, and deliberate movements to convey Scrooge's harshness. This portrayal harks back to the broader traditions of melodramatic storytelling prevalent in Dickens's time, where characters often embodied extreme virtues or vices for heightened emotional impact.

Nuanced Vulnerability:

Contrary to the traditional stern depiction, some adaptations opt for a more nuanced portrayal of Scrooge—one that explores the vulnerabilities beneath his harsh exterior. In these renditions, Scrooge is presented as a man burdened by the weight of his past choices, haunted by regrets and the ghosts of his youth. This interpretation humanizes Scrooge, inviting audiences to empathize with the complexities that have shaped him.

Actors portraying Scrooge with nuanced vulnerability often bring subtlety to their performances. Their facial expressions convey a conflict between the gruff exterior and glimpses of inner turmoil. The moments of solitude, where Scrooge reflects on his past or observes the lives of others, become poignant explorations of the character's internal struggles.

These portrayals delve into Scrooge's backstory, providing glimpses of his earlier life, lost loves, or moments that forged his path toward becoming the miserly figure audiences initially encounter. By unearthing the layers beneath the traditional portrayal, filmmakers aim to elicit not just sympathy but a profound understanding of Scrooge's humanity, making his redemption all the more compelling.

Humorous Eccentricity:

In certain adaptations, filmmakers take a departure from the stoic or tormented portrayals of Scrooge and infuse the character with a humorous eccentricity. This version of Scrooge is characterized by quirks, idiosyncrasies, and a lighthearted approach to his miserly tendencies. The humor in these portrayals often arises from the absurdity of Scrooge's behavior rather than the severity of his meanness.

Actors in these adaptations play up the comedic elements of Scrooge's personality, delivering lines with a wry wit and incorporating physical humor into their performances. This portrayal transforms Scrooge into a more approachable, albeit peculiar, figure whose miserliness becomes a source of amusement rather than dread.

The humorous eccentricity often extends to Scrooge's interactions with the supernatural elements of the story, making his encounters with the Ghosts of Christmas Past, Present, and Yet to Come comedic set pieces. This approach aims to engage audiences with a lighter and more whimsical interpretation of the character while retaining the essential elements of his transformation.

Aging and Frailty:

As an exploration of the aging process and mortality, some adaptations choose to portray Scrooge as not only miserly but also physically frail and vulnerable. In these renditions, Scrooge is presented as an elderly man who, in addition to confronting his past, must grapple with the inevitability of his own mortality. This choice adds an extra layer of poignancy to the character's journey of self-discovery.

Actors embodying the aging and frailty of Scrooge often use physicality to convey the toll of time. A shuffling gait, trembling hands, and a more fragile demeanor contribute to the portrayal of a man at the twilight of his life. This interpretation emphasizes the urgency of Scrooge's transformation, framing it not only as a moral awakening but also as a quest for redemption before it's too late.

The aging and frailty portrayal also underscores the vulnerability of Scrooge in the face of the supernatural, emphasizing the powerlessness of even the seemingly invulnerable when confronted with the mysteries of the afterlife. Through this lens, Scrooge's journey becomes a poignant meditation on the passage of time and the opportunity for change, no matter how late in life.

Contemporary Reimaginings:

In more contemporary reimaginings of "A Christmas Carol," filmmakers often take creative liberties with the character of Scrooge, updating his persona to align with modern sensibilities. These adaptations may place Scrooge in a different profession, recontextualize his wealth, or explore new facets of his personality that resonate with contemporary audiences.

Contemporary Scrooges may be CEOs of multinational corporations, tech moguls, or high-powered executives, reflecting societal shifts and concerns. This choice allows filmmakers to explore themes of corporate greed, income inequality, and the impact of modern capitalism while retaining the essential narrative structure of Dickens's tale.

The personalities of contemporary Scrooges may differ significantly from the traditional archetype. They could be charismatic yet cutthroat individuals, using charm and charisma to mask their underlying callousness. This approach challenges audiences to reconsider their preconceived notions of who Scrooge is and how he operates in a contemporary context.

Moreover, contemporary reimaginings may introduce new elements to Scrooge's character, such as technology dependence, environmental negligence, or other issues relevant to the present day. These adaptations aim to bridge the gap between Dickens's Victorian London and the contemporary world, presenting Scrooge as a figure whose flaws and redemptive journey remain pertinent across time.

Theatrical Extravaganza:

Some adaptations choose to embrace the theatricality inherent in Dickens's storytelling by presenting Scrooge as a larger-than-life figure. In these renditions, Scrooge's character is heightened to the point of becoming a theatrical spectacle—a magnetic and commanding presence whose every word and action reverberate with dramatic impact.

Actors embodying this theatrical extravagance often infuse their performances with grand gestures, booming voices, and a commanding stage presence. The portrayal of Scrooge becomes a tour de force, with each encounter and revelation unfolding like a scene from a grand theatrical production. This approach seeks to capture the essence of Dickens's original serialized storytelling, where each chapter was designed to captivate and enthrall readers.

The theatrical extravagance may extend to the supernatural elements of the story, with the Ghosts assuming larger-than-life forms and the environments they traverse becoming elaborate stage sets. This heightened theatricality aims to immerse audiences in a cinematic experience that mirrors the dramatic impact of Dickens's original narrative.

Conclusion:

The myriad portrayals of Ebenezer Scrooge across cinematic adaptations of "A Christmas Carol" showcase the character's enduring complexity and the interpretive freedom offered to filmmakers. Whether depicted with traditional sternness, nuanced vulnerability, humorous eccentricity, aging and frailty, contemporary reimaginings, or theatrical extravagance, Scrooge remains a timeless figure whose journey of redemption continues to resonate with audiences across generations. Through the lens of different actors and directors, the character of Scrooge becomes a canvas for exploring the human condition, the transformative power of empathy, and the enduring relevance of Dickens's classic tale in the ever-evolving landscape of cinema.

In the realm of Christmas tales, "A Christmas Carol" stands out as a narrative that weaves together the festive spirit of the season with an exploration of darker themes. The novella, penned by Charles Dickens in 1843, has been adapted countless times for the screen, with each interpretation grappling with the delicate balance of infusing holiday cheer while retaining the story's inherent darkness. In this exploration of the dark atmosphere and tone prevalent in cinematic adaptations of "A Christmas Carol," we delve into how filmmakers use visual and narrative elements to evoke a sense of foreboding, redemption, and the haunting specters of Scrooge's past, present, and future.

Establishing a Bleak Canvas:

Central to the dark atmosphere of "A Christmas Carol" is the setting—a bleak, wintry Victorian London. Filmmakers often employ stark visuals to depict a city shrouded in darkness, where the glow of gas lamps casts long shadows on cobblestone streets. The juxtaposition of icy breath in the air against the warmth of festively lit windows sets the stage for a narrative that unfolds on the cusp of joy and despair.

The darkened cityscape serves as a metaphor for the state of Scrooge's heart—cold, isolated, and resistant to the warmth of Christmas. By establishing this grim canvas, filmmakers immerse audiences in a world where the contrast between the festive season and the desolation of Scrooge's existence is palpable. The use of muted colors, such as deep blues and grays, contributes to the overall sense of melancholy, foreshadowing the transformative journey that lies ahead.

Eerie Soundscapes:

A crucial component of establishing a dark atmosphere in "A Christmas Carol" is the manipulation of sound. Filmmakers utilize eerie soundscapes to heighten the supernatural and haunting elements of the narrative. The distant wailing of the wind, creaking of floorboards, and the tolling of somber bells create an auditory backdrop that mirrors the emotional turbulence of Scrooge's encounters with the Ghosts.

The use of diegetic and non-diegetic sounds contributes to the overall sense of foreboding. Footsteps echoing in empty hallways, the rattling of chains, and ethereal whispers enhance the atmospheric tension. Even in moments of apparent tranquility, the subtle incorporation of unsettling sounds maintains a sense of unease, signaling that the specters of Christmas past, present, and future are always lurking in the shadows.

Musical scores in these adaptations often feature haunting melodies that evoke a sense of longing, regret, and the passage of time. Composers utilize minor key arrangements and dissonant chords to underscore the emotional weight of Scrooge's journey. The result is a haunting auditory experience that complements the visual bleakness, enveloping audiences in a world where the line between reality and the supernatural is blurred.

Ghosts as Agents of Darkness:

The three Ghosts of Christmas—Past, Present, and Yet to Come—are pivotal agents in shaping the dark atmosphere of "A Christmas Carol." These spectral entities serve as conduits for Scrooge's self-discovery and redemption, each representing a facet of his existence that he must confront. Filmmakers employ various visual and narrative techniques to render these ghosts as haunting and ethereal presences.

The Ghost of Christmas Past is often portrayed as a glowing, ephemeral figure that illuminates Scrooge's memories. The use of soft lighting and a gentle, nostalgic ambiance adds to the spectral quality of this entity. However, beneath the surface warmth, there's an inherent sadness as it guides Scrooge through moments of joy and sorrow, emphasizing the fleeting nature of time.

Conversely, the Ghost of Christmas Present is depicted as a more robust and jovial figure, adorned with festive regalia. Yet, even in its merriment, there is a sense of transience, as the spirit embodies the fleeting nature of the present moment. The juxtaposition of abundance and the inevitable withering away of holiday festivities contributes to the bittersweet atmosphere.

The Ghost of Christmas Yet to Come, often portrayed as a shadowy and foreboding figure, casts a chilling presence over the narrative. Its lack of a discernible face and the shrouded robe contribute to an aura of mystery and dread. Filmmakers manipulate lighting to accentuate the ghost's ominous nature, using shadows and dimly lit environments to evoke a sense of impending doom.

These spectral entities become conduits for exploring the darker corners of Scrooge's soul, guiding him through a journey that unearths repressed memories, confronts the consequences of his actions, and forces him to reckon with the inevitability of mortality. Through the visual portrayal of these ghosts, filmmakers emphasize that true redemption requires a confrontation with the darkness within.

Symbolism in Visual Metaphors:

The dark atmosphere of "A Christmas Carol" is often conveyed through symbolic visual metaphors that mirror Scrooge's internal struggles. Filmmakers employ these symbols to communicate themes of isolation, remorse, and the transformative power of redemption.

Chains are a recurring visual motif, symbolizing the weight of Scrooge's sins and the burden of his avarice. The clinking of chains, whether literal or symbolic, becomes a haunting reminder of the consequences of a life lived in pursuit of material wealth at the expense of human connection. As Scrooge encounters these chains in various forms, the visual metaphor reinforces the urgency of his redemption.

Mirrors and reflective surfaces serve as powerful visual metaphors for self-reflection and introspection. In moments of confrontation with the Ghosts, Scrooge is often compelled to gaze into mirrors that reveal his past, present, and potential future. These reflective surfaces become portals into the recesses of his own conscience, amplifying the psychological intensity of his journey.

The use of shadows and silhouettes contributes to the mysterious and ominous tone of the narrative. Filmmakers strategically position characters and objects in shadowy environments, heightening the sense of uncertainty and moral ambiguity. As Scrooge navigates through dimly lit spaces, the interplay of light and shadow becomes a visual representation of the internal conflict between darkness and the potential for enlightenment.

Similarly, the ticking of clocks and the representation of time as an ever-present force add to the dark atmosphere. The relentless march of time becomes a constant reminder of mortality and the finite nature of human existence. Filmmakers use visual cues such as pendulums swinging and hourglasses draining to accentuate the urgency of Scrooge's transformative journey.

Narrative Exploration of Darkness:

Beyond visual and auditory elements, the dark atmosphere of "A Christmas Carol" is deeply ingrained in the narrative exploration of darkness—both literal and metaphorical. The narrative traverses the shadows of Scrooge's past, the stark realities of the present, and the ominous uncertainties of the future.

The Ghost of Christmas Past delves into Scrooge's childhood, unraveling the roots of his bitterness and isolation. The repressed memories that surface during this journey become a narrative exploration of the darkness that has shaped Scrooge's psyche. From his estrangement from family to the loss of love, the past becomes a haunting landscape of regrets and missed opportunities.

The Ghost of Christmas Present exposes Scrooge to the harsh realities of the world around him. Scenes of poverty, hardship, and the Cratchit family's struggles provide a stark contrast to the festivities outside Scrooge's own window. The juxtaposition of joy and suffering becomes a narrative exploration of societal darkness, prompting Scrooge to confront the consequences of his own indifference.

The climax of darkness occurs with the Ghost of Christmas Yet to Come, who guides Scrooge through a future bereft of hope. The narrative unfolds in a world where the absence of Scrooge's compassion has led to tragic outcomes. The death of Tiny Tim and the isolation of Scrooge in death become potent narrative devices that force Scrooge to confront the ultimate darkness that awaits him if he does not change.

The narrative arc of "A Christmas Carol" is inherently a journey from darkness to light, with Scrooge's redemption serving as the guiding force. The exploration of darkness becomes a narrative tool that heightens the emotional stakes, making the eventual transformation and embrace of the Christmas spirit all the more impactful.

Redemption Through Contrast:

The dark atmosphere of "A Christmas Carol" serves a dual purpose—it accentuates the severity of Scrooge's initial state and provides a stark backdrop against which his redemption can unfold. Filmmakers strategically use contrast to amplify the transformative nature of Scrooge's journey, emphasizing the impact of his newfound empathy and generosity against the darkness that pervaded his life.

The contrast is evident in the visual transformation of Scrooge's surroundings. As he awakens on Christmas morning, the once desolate and dimly lit spaces of his home are bathed in warm, golden light. The previously somber and muted colors give way to vibrant hues, symbolizing the infusion of joy and compassion into Scrooge's world.

The contrast extends to Scrooge's interactions with others. His once dismissive and callous demeanor is replaced by acts of kindness and generosity. The change in his relationships, particularly with the Cratchit family, becomes a powerful narrative device that highlights the impact of embracing the Christmas spirit. Scenes of shared laughter, festive meals, and heartfelt connections stand in stark contrast to the loneliness and isolation that characterized Scrooge's earlier interactions.

The transformation is also reflected in Scrooge's own appearance. His countenance, once etched with severity, evolves into a visage of warmth and genuine emotion. The joyous glint in his eyes, the infectiousness of his laughter, and the sincerity of his actions become visual cues that underscore the magnitude of his redemption.

By utilizing contrast, filmmakers amplify the emotional resonance of Scrooge's redemption. The stark shift from darkness to light becomes a visual and narrative metaphor for the potential for change, even in the bleakest of circumstances. The contrast reinforces the central message of "A Christmas

Carol"—that the human capacity for redemption and transformation is boundless, and that even the darkest hearts can find solace in the embrace of compassion.

Conclusion:

The dark atmosphere and tone prevalent in cinematic adaptations of "A Christmas Carol" serve as integral elements that elevate the narrative beyond a simple holiday tale. Through visual and auditory techniques, symbolism, and narrative exploration, filmmakers craft a world where the juxtaposition of darkness and light becomes a canvas for Scrooge's transformative journey. The haunting specters of the past, present, and future, coupled with the atmospheric richness of a wintry Victorian London, create an immersive experience that resonates with audiences, inviting them to confront the shadows within and embrace the enduring message of redemption and goodwill. In the darkness of Scrooge's world, the flicker of a candle becomes a symbol of hope, and the journey from despair to joy becomes a timeless exploration of the human spirit's capacity for change.

"A Christmas Carol," Charles Dickens's timeless novella, has not only left an indelible mark on literature and cinema but has also significantly influenced and contributed to shaping holiday traditions around the world. The story's themes of generosity, redemption, and the transformative power of empathy have resonated with audiences for nearly two centuries, and its impact extends beyond the realm of entertainment into the very fabric of how we celebrate Christmas. In this exploration of the "Impact on Holiday Traditions," we delve into the ways in which "A Christmas Carol" has shaped and enriched the festive season for generations.

The Birth of Christmas as We Know It:

One of the most profound impacts of "A Christmas Carol" on holiday traditions is its role in shaping the modern celebration of Christmas. In the mid-19th century, when Dickens penned his novella, Christmas in England was undergoing a transformation. The Industrial Revolution had led to social and economic changes, and the holiday had lost some of its traditional significance. Dickens, with his heartfelt portrayal of Scrooge's redemption and the joyous celebrations of the Cratchit family, played a pivotal role in rekindling the spirit of Christmas.

The story's emphasis on compassion, kindness, and the importance of human connection struck a chord with Victorian readers. Dickens's vivid descriptions of festive decorations, feasts, and communal celebrations reinvigorated interest in

Christmas traditions that were on the verge of fading away. "A Christmas Carol" became a cultural touchstone that reminded people of the true meaning of Christmas—a time for generosity, reflection, and togetherness.

Popularizing Christmas Trees and Decorations:

One of the enduring symbols of Christmas that "A Christmas Carol" helped popularize is the Christmas tree. In the story, as Scrooge undergoes his transformation, he witnesses the Cratchit family joyfully preparing for Christmas, complete with a festive tree adorned with ornaments. This depiction contributed to the growing popularity of Christmas trees in Victorian England and, later, around the world.

The image of a beautifully decorated tree, with lights and ornaments, became ingrained in the public's perception of a festive Christmas celebration. The tradition of bringing an evergreen tree into the home and adorning it with lights and decorations became a widespread practice. The Cratchit family's modest yet heartfelt celebration, as described by Dickens, resonated with readers and inspired them to incorporate similar elements into their own holiday traditions.

The Spirit of Giving and Generosity:

Perhaps the most enduring legacy of "A Christmas Carol" on holiday traditions is its emphasis on the spirit of giving and generosity. The story imparts a powerful message about the joy of helping others, being compassionate, and extending a helping hand to those in need. Scrooge's transformation from a miserly and self-centered individual to a benevolent and caring benefactor serves as a timeless reminder of the true spirit of Christmas.

In the wake of the novella's success, charitable giving during the holiday season gained prominence. Inspired by Scrooge's redemption, individuals and organizations began to embrace the idea of giving back to their communities. The themes of charity and goodwill embedded in "A Christmas Carol" influenced the tradition of giving gifts during the holiday season, with an emphasis on thoughtful and meaningful presents that foster a sense of connection and generosity.

Influence on Christmas Caroling:

The tradition of Christmas caroling, where groups of people go door to door singing festive songs, also owes a debt to "A Christmas Carol." The Cratchit family's joyful singing on Christmas Day, despite their humble circumstances, highlighted the transformative power of music and communal celebration. This depiction resonated with readers and contributed to the popularization of caroling as a cherished holiday activity.

The themes of togetherness and spreading joy through song became integral to the Christmas caroling tradition. The spirit of caroling aligns with Dickens's vision of Christmas as a time for shared merriment and the uplifting power of music. Today, caroling remains a beloved holiday tradition that brings communities together in the shared joy of festive melodies.

Culinary Traditions and Feasting:

The lavish descriptions of the Cratchit family's Christmas feast in "A Christmas Carol" have left an imprint on culinary traditions associated with the holiday season. The novella paints a vivid picture of a bountiful table with a roast goose, Christmas pudding, and other delectable treats. Dickens's evocative descriptions of festive meals have inspired generations to create their own elaborate holiday feasts.

The emphasis on sharing a hearty meal with loved ones, regardless of one's economic circumstances, has become a central theme in Christmas celebrations. Families often gather around the table to partake in a festive feast reminiscent of the Cratchit family's Christmas dinner. Traditional holiday foods like roast turkey, ham, and Christmas pudding continue to be enjoyed in households worldwide, thanks in part to the enduring influence of "A Christmas Carol."

Adaptations as Annual Tradition:

As "A Christmas Carol" became a cultural phenomenon, the tradition of adapting and performing the story as a play or film during the holiday season emerged. Many theaters and production companies worldwide make staging or screening an adaptation of "A Christmas Carol" an annual tradition. These performances, ranging from faithful renditions to creative reinterpretations, have become a staple of the holiday entertainment calendar.

Countless actors have taken on the iconic role of Ebenezer Scrooge, bringing their unique interpretations to the character. Families and communities often make it a tradition to attend or watch a performance of "A Christmas Carol" during the holiday season, reinforcing the story's enduring impact on festive entertainment.

Educational and Moral Lessons:

Beyond its influence on specific traditions, "A Christmas Carol" has become a vehicle for imparting moral and educational lessons during the holiday season. The story's exploration of themes such as empathy, compassion, and the consequences of avarice provides a valuable framework for discussions about values and character.

Educators often incorporate the novella into holiday-themed curricula, using Scrooge's journey as a means to engage students in discussions about morality, redemption, and the importance of social responsibility. The timeless nature of the story makes it a versatile tool for fostering ethical reflections and encouraging individuals to consider how they can contribute positively to their communities.

Inspiration for Contemporary Media:

The impact of "A Christmas Carol" extends beyond literature and live performances to influence contemporary media. Countless film adaptations, television specials, and animated features continue to draw inspiration from Dickens's novella, creating a continuous stream of reinterpretations that resonate with new generations.

The enduring popularity of Scrooge's character and the universal themes explored in "A Christmas Carol" ensure that its influence will persist in contemporary storytelling. The story's adaptability to different mediums allows it to reach diverse audiences, ensuring that the lessons of compassion and redemption remain relevant in a modern context.

Conclusion:

"A Christmas Carol" stands as a literary masterpiece that transcends its status as a seasonal tale to become a transformative force in shaping holiday traditions. From popularizing Christmas trees and decorations to influencing charitable giving and inspiring annual adaptations, Dickens's novella has left an indelible mark on how we celebrate Christmas. Its enduring legacy lies not only in the rich tapestry of festive customs but also in the moral and emotional resonance that continues to define the holiday season for millions around the world. As families gather, feasts are shared, and acts of kindness abound, the spirit of "A Christmas Carol" lives on, reminding us all of the profound impact of generosity, compassion, and the true meaning of Christmas.

Chapter 4 - How the Grinch Stole Christmas (2000) Jim Carrey's Manic Performance

In the realm of holiday classics, few characters are as iconic and beloved as Dr. Seuss's Grinch. When Ron Howard took on the ambitious task of bringing "How the Grinch Stole Christmas" to the big screen in 2000, the casting of Jim Carrey as the titular character added a layer of manic energy and comedic brilliance that left an indelible mark on the film. Carrey's portrayal of the Grinch is a masterclass in physical comedy, facial expressions, and improvisational talent, elevating the character from a two-dimensional villain to a complex, endearing, and ultimately heartwarming figure. In this exploration of "Jim Carrey's Manic Performance," we delve into the nuances of Carrey's transformative portrayal and its impact on the enduring appeal of this festive cinematic adaptation.

The Challenge of Adapting Dr. Seuss:

Bringing a Dr. Seuss character to life on the big screen is a task laden with challenges. Seuss's whimsical and fantastical worlds, populated by uniquely shaped characters and surreal landscapes, pose a creative puzzle for filmmakers. When it came to translating the Grinch from the pages of the beloved children's book to a live-action film, the casting of Jim Carrey brought a dynamic and unpredictable element to the mix.

The Grinch, with his green fur, mischievous grin, and disdain for all things Christmas, presented an opportunity for an actor to not just wear the costume but fully inhabit the character. Jim Carrey, known for his elastic facial expressions, physical comedy prowess, and over-the-top comedic style, proved to be the perfect choice to take on the challenge of personifying the Grinch's larger-than-life personality.

Carrey's Physical Transformation:

Jim Carrey is no stranger to physical transformations for his roles, and his embodiment of the Grinch is a testament to his dedication to the craft. The elaborate makeup and prosthetics used to turn Carrey into the furry, green recluse were crucial in bringing the fantastical character to life. The intricate details of the Grinch's appearance, from his twisted smile to his wild, untamed hair, were meticulously crafted to capture the essence of Dr. Seuss's original creation.

Carrey's physicality in the role is nothing short of remarkable. The Grinch's exaggerated movements, from his slinking and skulking to his high-energy antics, mirror Carrey's own brand of physical comedy. The actor's commitment to embodying the Grinch's peculiar mannerisms adds a layer of authenticity to the character, allowing audiences to suspend disbelief and fully immerse themselves in the fantastical world of Whoville.

Facial Expressions as a Narrative Tool:

One of Jim Carrey's most potent tools in his portrayal of the Grinch is his expressive face. The intricate makeup and prosthetics, while essential in creating the visual transformation, could easily have hindered an actor's ability to convey nuanced emotions. However, Carrey skillfully utilizes his facial expressions as a narrative tool, allowing the audience to glimpse the Grinch's complex range of emotions.

From the Grinch's initial distaste for all things Christmas to his gradual transformation into a character capable of experiencing joy and connection, Carrey's facial expressions serve as a window into the character's evolving emotional landscape. The twinkle in his eye during moments of mischief, the furrowed brow of contemplation, and the infectious grin of genuine happiness all contribute to the Grinch's multidimensional persona.

The ability to convey subtle emotions through layers of makeup and prosthetics is a testament to Carrey's mastery of his craft. It is through these nuanced facial expressions that the Grinch transcends the realm of a mere antagonist and becomes a relatable and ultimately sympathetic character.

Manic Energy and Improvisational Brilliance:

Jim Carrey's comedic style is often characterized by a manic energy that propels his performances to comedic heights. This energy is on full display in his portrayal of the Grinch. The character's mischievous antics, frenetic movements, and unpredictable behavior align seamlessly with Carrey's own brand of physical and improvisational comedy.

Throughout the film, Carrey infuses the Grinch with a lively and unpredictable energy that keeps audiences engaged and entertained. From his chaotic interactions with the residents of Whoville to his solo moments of revelry and mischief, Carrey's performance channels the anarchic spirit of Dr. Seuss's original creation. The Grinch becomes a conduit for Carrey's improvisational brilliance, with the actor bringing his unique comedic sensibilities to each scene.

Carrey's improvisational skills are particularly evident in moments of dialogue and physical comedy. Whether engaging in witty banter with other characters or delivering monologues in the solitude of his mountaintop lair, Carrey's ability to think on his feet and inject spontaneity into his performance adds a layer of unpredictability to the character. The Grinch's interactions with his canine companion, Max, are particularly notable for the seamless interplay between scripted dialogue and Carrey's ad-libbed moments.

Balancing Comedy and Heart:

While Carrey's performance as the Grinch is undeniably comedic and often over-the-top, what elevates it to a truly memorable level is the underlying sense of heart that he brings to the character. Despite the Grinch's initial disdain for Christmas and his isolated existence atop Mount Crumpit, Carrey infuses the character with moments of vulnerability, introspection, and, ultimately, redemption.

The Grinch's journey from a cantankerous loner to a character capable of embracing the spirit of Christmas hinges on the emotional depth that Carrey brings to the role. Moments of self-reflection, conveyed through both dialogue and expressive physicality, allow the audience to empathize with the Grinch's internal struggles. Carrey strikes a delicate balance between comedy and genuine emotion, ensuring that the character's transformation feels earned and resonant.

The film's narrative arc, which explores the Grinch's backstory and the reasons behind his disdain for Christmas, benefits immensely from Carrey's ability to convey a complex range of emotions. The actor's commitment to portraying the Grinch as a multifaceted character adds a layer of depth that goes beyond the surface-level comedy often associated with holiday films.

Impact on the Film's Enduring Appeal:

Jim Carrey's manic performance as the Grinch is a key factor in the enduring appeal of Ron Howard's cinematic adaptation of "How the Grinch Stole Christmas." The film, released over two decades ago, continues to be a holiday staple for audiences of all ages. Carrey's portrayal of the Grinch has become synonymous with the character itself, with many viewers citing his performance as a highlight of the film.

The Grinch's character arc, from a curmudgeonly recluse to a symbol of redemption and communal celebration, is made all the more memorable through Carrey's transformative performance. The actor's ability to elicit laughter, evoke empathy, and convey genuine emotion contributes to the film's timeless quality. The Grinch, as portrayed by Carrey, has become an enduring symbol of the redemptive power of love, kindness, and the spirit of Christmas.

Cultural Impact and Legacy:

Beyond the immediate success of the film, Jim Carrey's performance as the Grinch has had a lasting cultural impact. The character has become a pop culture icon, with references and parodies permeating holiday-themed media and entertainment. Carrey's distinctive portrayal has set a benchmark for future adaptations of the Grinch character, and subsequent actors taking on the role are inevitably compared to his iconic interpretation.

The film's enduring popularity is reflected in its continued presence in holiday programming, merchandise, and cultural discussions surrounding Christmas films. Carrey's Grinch has transcended the boundaries of the screen to become an integral part of the collective holiday experience for audiences around the world.

Conclusion:

Jim Carrey's manic performance as the Grinch in Ron Howard's "How the Grinch Stole Christmas" is a testament to the transformative power of a skilled actor. Carrey not only brought Dr. Seuss's iconic character to life but added layers of depth, humor, and heart to the role. Through his physicality, facial expressions, improvisational brilliance, and the delicate balance of comedy and emotion, Carrey elevated the Grinch from a simple antagonist to a complex and endearing figure. The enduring appeal of the film, even decades after its release, is a testament to the cultural impact of Carrey's portrayal and the indelible mark it has left on the holiday film genre. In the pantheon of Christmas classics, Carrey's Grinch stands as a shining example of how a truly transformative performance can elevate a beloved character to iconic status.

In the realm of holiday cinema, few tales are as universally cherished as Dr. Seuss's "How the Grinch Stole Christmas." Ron Howard's 2000 cinematic adaptation brought the whimsical world of Whoville to life in a visually stunning manner. Central to the film's success was its whimsical production design, which skillfully translated Seuss's distinctive illustrations into a vibrant and immersive three-dimensional setting. In this exploration of "Whimsical Production Design Elements," we delve into the creative choices, visual aesthetics, and cinematic techniques that contributed to the enchanting world of Whoville and played a pivotal role in the film's enduring appeal.

Translating Seuss's Whimsy to the Screen:

Adapting the whimsical and fantastical world created by Dr. Seuss presented a unique set of challenges and opportunities for the filmmakers. Seuss's illustrations, characterized by their playful shapes, vibrant colors, and fantastical landscapes, are an integral part of the charm that defines his stories. Ron Howard, along with production designer Michael Corenblith, faced the task of translating this distinctive visual style to the cinematic medium while retaining the essence of Seuss's whimsy.

One of the most notable design choices was the decision to recreate Whoville as a practical set rather than relying extensively on CGI. The physicality of the set, with its curved architecture, crooked buildings, and exaggerated proportions, mirrored the curvature and playfulness found in Seuss's original illustrations. This approach not only paid homage to Seuss's visual style but also provided actors and audiences with a tangible and immersive environment.

Curved Architecture and Playful Proportions:

Whoville's architecture serves as a visual testament to the film's commitment to capturing Seuss's whimsical aesthetic. The buildings in Whoville are characterized by their curved lines, unconventional shapes, and exaggerated proportions. The decision to embrace these playful architectural elements adds a sense of fantastical realism to the setting, creating a world that feels both familiar and delightfully surreal.

The curvature of the buildings, often leaning at whimsical angles, reflects the organic and free-flowing nature of Seuss's illustrations. Rather than adhering to traditional geometric structures, the filmmakers embraced irregular shapes and playful asymmetry. This design choice not only aligns with Seuss's visual language but also contributes to the overall sense of whimsy that permeates Whoville.

The exaggerated proportions of Whoville's architecture extend beyond mere visual aesthetics—they play a crucial role in reinforcing the film's thematic elements. The larger-than-life structures symbolize the larger-than-life spirit of the Whos, emphasizing their capacity for joy, resilience, and a celebration of the holiday season despite the Grinch's attempts to steal Christmas.

Vibrant Color Palette:

Color plays a pivotal role in Dr. Seuss's storytelling, and the film adaptation of "How the Grinch Stole Christmas" embraced a vibrant and saturated palette to bring Whoville to life. The use of bold and bright colors, reminiscent of Seuss's original illustrations, contributes to the film's whimsical atmosphere and visual richness.

Each building in Whoville is painted in an array of vivid hues, creating a kaleidoscopic landscape that mirrors the joyous and festive nature of the Whos. The filmmakers carefully selected colors that not only captured the spirit of Seuss's illustrations but also conveyed a sense of warmth, community, and holiday cheer. The juxtaposition of vibrant buildings against the snowy backdrop of Mount Crumpit creates a visual feast that immerses the audience in the magical world of Whoville.

Beyond the buildings, the film's costume design also adheres to a lively color palette. The Whos' clothing features a mix of patterns, textures, and bright colors, contributing to the overall visual spectacle. This intentional choice in color coordination serves as a visual cue for the audience, reinforcing the film's central theme of the Whos' unwavering commitment to the spirit of Christmas.

Surreal Landscapes and Cinematic Magic:

The film's whimsical production design extends beyond Whoville to encompass the surreal landscapes surrounding the town. From the snow-covered slopes of Mount Crumpit to the fantastical machinery of the Grinch's lair, every environment in the film is crafted with meticulous attention to detail and a touch of cinematic magic.

The snow-covered Mount Crumpit, where the Grinch resides, serves as a visual contrast to the vibrant colors of Whoville. The filmmakers used a combination of practical effects and CGI to create a snowy landscape that captures the enchanting and slightly surreal quality of Seuss's illustrations. The use of practical snow, combined with carefully designed sets, contributes to the film's tactile and immersive quality.

The Grinch's lair itself is a marvel of whimsical production design. The fantastical machinery and contraptions within the lair, including the iconic sleigh and bag-stealing apparatus, reflect the Grinch's eccentric and inventive nature. The use of oversized gears, pulleys, and levers adds a touch of steampunk-inspired whimsy to the environment, reinforcing the film's commitment to creating a visually captivating world.

Costume Design and Character Aesthetics:

In addition to the architectural and environmental design elements, the film's costume design plays a crucial role in establishing the whimsical atmosphere of Whoville. The inhabitants of Whoville, known as the Whos, are characterized by their distinctive clothing, which mirrors the playful and eclectic nature of Seuss's illustrations.

The costume design embraces a mix of textures, patterns, and unconventional accessories to create a visually dynamic ensemble for each character. From Mayor Augustus Maywho's flamboyant outfits to Cindy Lou Who's endearing simplicity, every costume reflects the individual personalities of the Whos. The use of exaggerated accessories, such as oversized bows and distinctive headwear, contributes to the film's overall sense of whimsy.

The Grinch's costume, a faithful recreation of Seuss's original depiction, is a standout element of the film's character design. Jim Carrey's transformation into the Grinch is complemented by the intricate makeup and prosthetics that capture the character's iconic appearance. The decision to stay true to Seuss's illustrations in both costume and makeup design ensures a seamless integration of the Grinch into the whimsical world of Whoville.

Incorporating Seussian Elements:

To fully capture the essence of Dr. Seuss's whimsical world, the filmmakers incorporated distinct Seussian elements into the production design. Seuss's illustrations are characterized by playful shapes, fanciful landscapes, and imaginative flora and fauna. The film's production design team meticulously recreated these elements, infusing the settings with a sense of otherworldly charm.

The film features Seussian trees with unconventional shapes, whimsical flowers, and fantastical plant life that defy the norms of the natural world. These elements, while visually surreal, contribute to the film's overall sense of magic and wonder. The decision to embrace Seussian aesthetics extends to every corner of Whoville, creating an environment that feels plucked from the pages of a storybook.

Incorporating Seussian elements also extended to the film's use of visual effects. CGI was employed to bring to life some of the more fantastical and gravity-defying elements of

Seuss's illustrations, ensuring that the film remained faithful to the source material while leveraging the capabilities of modern filmmaking technology.

The Cinematic Experience of Whoville:

The whimsical production design of "How the Grinch Stole Christmas" extends beyond mere visual aesthetics; it contributes to the overall cinematic experience of Whoville. The careful consideration of architectural details, color palettes, and Seussian elements creates a world that feels both fantastical and lived-in. As the camera navigates the curved streets of Whoville and explores the nooks and crannies of the Grinch's lair, the audience is invited into a cinematic realm that transcends the boundaries of traditional set design.

The choice to build practical sets, rather than relying solely on CGI, adds a tactile and tangible quality to the film's environments. Audiences can almost feel the whimsical curvature of the buildings, sense the crunch of snow beneath their feet, and marvel at the larger-than-life machinery within the Grinch's lair. This immersive quality enhances the storytelling, allowing viewers to fully engage with the fantastical world on screen.

Legacy and Continued Influence:

The whimsical production design of "How the Grinch Stole Christmas" has left an enduring legacy in the realm of holiday cinema. The film's visual aesthetics, commitment to Seussian whimsy, and immersive environments have set a standard for subsequent adaptations and holiday-themed films. Whoville, as brought to life by Ron Howard and his team, remains an iconic and instantly recognizable setting that continues to captivate audiences of all ages.

The enduring popularity of the film, even years after its initial release, speaks to the timeless appeal of its production design. Whoville has become synonymous with the magic and joy of the holiday season, and its whimsical landscapes have left an indelible mark on the collective imagination of audiences around the world.

The film's success in translating Seuss's visual language to the cinematic medium has influenced subsequent adaptations of the author's works and set a precedent for bringing beloved children's stories to life on the big screen. Filmmakers undertaking the challenge of adapting Seussian tales must reckon with the high standard set by "How the Grinch Stole Christmas" in terms of production design and visual storytelling.

Conclusion:

In the enchanting world of "How the Grinch Stole Christmas," the whimsical production design stands as a testament to the creative ingenuity of the filmmakers. Through curved architecture, vibrant color palettes, surreal landscapes, and a commitment to Seussian aesthetics, Ron Howard and his team brought Dr. Seuss's vision to life in a cinematic masterpiece. Whoville, with its playful shapes and fantastical environments, became a tangible and immersive setting that continues to captivate audiences during the holiday season. The film's enduring legacy lies not only in its heartfelt narrative but also in the whimsical visual tapestry that has become synonymous with the magic and wonder of Christmas. In the pantheon of holiday classics, "How the Grinch Stole Christmas" stands as a shining example of the transformative power of whimsical production design in creating timeless cinematic experiences.

Kid-Friendly Christmas Vibes

In the heart of holiday cinema, few films capture the essence of Christmas with the same whimsy and charm as "How the Grinch Stole Christmas." Ron Howard's 2000 adaptation of Dr. Seuss's beloved tale not only brought the iconic character to life but also infused the narrative with kid-friendly Christmas vibes that resonate across generations. In this exploration of "Kid-Friendly Christmas Vibes," we delve into the enchanting world of Whoville, the endearing characters, and the timeless elements of the film that make it a perennial favorite for families during the holiday season.

Whoville's Magical Atmosphere:

At the core of the film's kid-friendly Christmas vibes is the magical atmosphere of Whoville itself. From the moment the film opens, audiences are transported to a fantastical world filled with whimsical architecture, vibrant colors, and a palpable sense of joy and celebration. Whoville serves as the perfect backdrop for a kid-friendly Christmas tale, offering a visual feast of delights that captures the imagination.

The town's curved streets, crooked buildings, and towering Christmas trees create a sense of wonder that is inherently appealing to children. The exaggerated and playful architecture of Whoville mirrors the kind of setting one might find in a child's storybook, where reality is skewed in delightful ways. This architectural whimsy sets the stage for a holiday adventure that unfolds in a landscape where anything seems possible.

The film's commitment to practical sets, rather than extensive use of CGI, enhances the tangible and immersive quality of Whoville. For young viewers, being able to see and believe in the physicality of the environment adds to the magic of the storytelling. Whoville becomes a place that feels not only visually enchanting but also one that children can almost reach out and touch.

Colorful Characters and Whimsical Costumes:

Kid-friendly Christmas vibes are further heightened by the colorful and endearing characters that populate Whoville. From the energetic and optimistic Cindy Lou Who to the boisterous Mayor Augustus Maywho, each character is brought to life with a distinct personality and visual flair. The costumes, in particular, play a crucial role in establishing the whimsical and kid-friendly atmosphere of the film.

Costume designer Rita Ryack embraced a vibrant and eclectic color palette for the Whos' attire. The characters' clothing is a delightful mix of patterns, textures, and unconventional accessories, reflecting the lively spirit of Whoville. For children, the visual spectacle of the characters' costumes adds an extra layer of excitement, turning each interaction into a colorful and whimsical experience.

The Grinch's iconic costume, complete with its green fur, Santa suit, and distinctive accessories, serves as a visual anchor for the film's Christmas theme. Jim Carrey's transformation into the Grinch is not only a testament to the actor's commitment but also a source of fascination for young audiences. The character's appearance strikes a balance between being slightly menacing and ultimately endearing, creating a captivating figure that captures the imagination of children.

Holiday Traditions and Festive Cheer:

At the heart of the film's kid-friendly Christmas vibes are the holiday traditions and festive cheer that permeate Whoville. The Whos are portrayed as a close-knit and joyous community that wholeheartedly embraces the spirit of Christmas. For children, the depiction of communal celebrations, cheerful gatherings, and festive rituals creates a sense of warmth and togetherness that aligns with their own experiences of the holiday season.

The film takes care to showcase various holiday traditions within Whoville, from tree decorating to gift-giving to singing. These familiar elements of Christmas resonate with young viewers, providing a cinematic representation of the rituals they associate with the holiday. The Whos' enthusiastic participation in these traditions becomes infectious, inviting children to immerse themselves in the joyous spirit of the season.

The iconic scene where the Whos join hands and sing "Welcome Christmas" is a powerful moment that encapsulates the film's celebration of togetherness and the true meaning of the holiday. The communal singing, accompanied by the twinkling lights of Whoville, creates a visual and auditory spectacle that evokes the magic of Christmas. For children, this moment becomes a cinematic embodiment of the joyous gatherings that define their own holiday experiences.

Cindy Lou Who's Heartwarming Journey:

A key element of the kid-friendly Christmas vibes in "How the Grinch Stole Christmas" is the heartwarming journey of Cindy Lou Who. Positioned as the film's moral compass, Cindy Lou's innocence, compassion, and determination to understand the true meaning of Christmas resonate deeply with young audiences. Her character arc serves as a relatable and empowering narrative for children.

Cindy Lou's curiosity about the Grinch and her desire to question the conventional narrative surrounding him reflect a child's natural inclination to seek understanding and empathy. For children, Cindy Lou becomes an accessible and relatable protagonist who embarks on a journey of self-discovery and compassion. Her character encourages young viewers to look beyond surface appearances and embrace the values of kindness and understanding.

The film's portrayal of Cindy Lou's interactions with the Grinch adds an emotional layer to the narrative. The Grinch, initially perceived as a menacing figure, is gradually humanized through Cindy Lou's eyes. Her unwavering belief in the goodness within the Grinch becomes a powerful message for children about the transformative power of empathy and compassion.

Cindy Lou's resilience in the face of adversity, her commitment to spreading joy, and her genuine belief in the Christmas spirit contribute to the film's overall kid-friendly vibes. Her character embodies the idea that even the grumpiest of individuals can experience redemption and that the true magic of Christmas lies in the capacity for love and generosity.

The Grinch's Redemption and Lesson in Giving:

At the heart of the film's kid-friendly Christmas narrative is the redemption arc of the Grinch himself. Driven by his initial disdain for Christmas and a misguided belief that material possessions define the holiday, the Grinch undergoes a transformative journey that resonates with young audiences.

The revelation that Christmas is about more than just presents becomes a poignant lesson for children. The Grinch's change of heart, fueled by witnessing the Whos' joyous celebrations despite the absence of material gifts, reinforces the idea that the true spirit of Christmas lies in love, togetherness, and giving. For children, this narrative element becomes a gentle reminder of the values that make the holiday season special.

The climactic scene where the Grinch's heart grows three sizes encapsulates the film's core message of redemption and personal growth. This visual metaphor becomes a powerful and memorable image for children, illustrating the transformative impact of embracing the true meaning of Christmas. The Grinch's shift from a character motivated by selfishness to one capable of selfless generosity resonates with young viewers, fostering a sense of hope and belief in the goodness within everyone.

Jim Carrey's portrayal of the Grinch adds a comedic and endearing layer to the character's redemption. The film balances moments of humor with genuine emotional resonance, ensuring that the Grinch's journey remains accessible and relatable for children. The incorporation of humor, coupled with the heartfelt moments of redemption, contributes to the overall kid-friendly tone of the narrative.

Humor and Physical Comedy for All Ages:

A hallmark of the film's kid-friendly Christmas vibes is its infusion of humor and physical comedy that appeals to audiences of all ages. Jim Carrey's energetic and comedic performance as the Grinch introduces a playful and entertaining element that resonates with children while maintaining broader appeal. The film skillfully navigates between moments of slapstick humor and heartfelt sincerity, creating a narrative that engages viewers on multiple levels.

The Grinch's antics, from his exaggerated expressions to his comically elaborate schemes, inject a sense of levity into the storytelling. For children, these moments of humor become memorable and enjoyable, offering laughter alongside the film's deeper themes. Carrey's physical comedy, characterized by expressive facial contortions and agile movements, adds a layer of entertainment that transcends generational boundaries.

The film's humor extends to other characters as well, with comedic moments woven into the fabric of Whoville's festive celebrations. Mayor Augustus Maywho's enthusiastic and theatrical demeanor, along with the antics of various Whos, contributes to the overall lighthearted tone. The inclusion of humor throughout the narrative ensures that the film remains accessible and engaging for young audiences, making it a joyful and entertaining holiday experience.

Musical Score and Whimsical Soundtrack:

The kid-friendly Christmas vibes of "How the Grinch Stole Christmas" are further accentuated by the film's musical score and whimsical soundtrack. Composer James Horner's contribution to the film's audio landscape enhances the emotional beats, heightens the comedic moments, and immerses viewers in the festive atmosphere of Whoville.

The iconic musical themes, including the playful and uplifting "Welcome Christmas" and the mischievous tones of the Grinch's leitmotif, become integral elements of the film's identity. For children, the infectious melodies and catchy tunes add to the overall sensory experience, creating a connection between the auditory and visual elements of the storytelling.

The film's musical sequences, such as the Whos' communal singing and the Grinch's own musical moments, contribute to the whimsical and joyous atmosphere. The use of music as a narrative tool reinforces the film's celebration of togetherness and the transformative power of the holiday spirit. The whimsical soundtrack becomes a festive backdrop that enhances the overall kid-friendly Christmas vibes, making the film a complete sensory delight.

Legacy and Enduring Appeal:

The kid-friendly Christmas vibes of "How the Grinch Stole Christmas" have cemented its status as a timeless holiday classic. The film's ability to capture the magic of Christmas through whimsical visuals, endearing characters, and heartfelt storytelling ensures its continued appeal for new generations of viewers. Whoville's enchanting world, the iconic characters, and the film's core messages of love, compassion, and the true meaning of Christmas create an enduring legacy that transcends the passage of time.

For families, the film has become a cherished part of their holiday traditions, with each viewing offering a festive and heartwarming experience. The Grinch, once perceived as a holiday antagonist, has been embraced as a symbol of redemption and the capacity for positive change. The film's ability to blend humor, sincerity, and magical storytelling makes it a perennial favorite for children and adults alike.

As a cinematic adaptation of a beloved children's book, "How the Grinch Stole Christmas" successfully captures the essence of Dr. Seuss's whimsical world while adding its own layer of cinematic magic. The film's enduring popularity during the holiday season speaks to its ability to evoke a sense of wonder and joy in audiences of all ages. Whether experienced as a nostalgic tradition or as a new discovery, the kid-friendly Christmas vibes of the Grinch continue to bring smiles and warmth to countless households each December.

Conclusion:

In the enchanting tapestry of holiday cinema, "How the Grinch Stole Christmas" stands as a shining example of kid-friendly Christmas vibes done right. From the whimsical landscapes of Whoville to the endearing characters, heartfelt messages, and festive celebrations, the film captures the magic and wonder of the holiday season. Through the eyes of Cindy Lou Who, the transformative journey of the Grinch, and the infusion of humor and music, the film creates a cinematic experience that resonates with young viewers and their families. As a timeless classic that continues to brighten the holiday season, "How the Grinch Stole Christmas" embodies the spirit of Christmas in a way that transcends generations, making it a beloved and enduring gem in the pantheon of festive films.

In the realm of holiday cinema, "How the Grinch Stole Christmas" emerged not only as a festive classic but also as a box office juggernaut. Ron Howard's 2000 adaptation of Dr. Seuss's beloved tale not only captured the hearts of audiences but also demonstrated the commercial appeal of a well-crafted Christmas narrative. In this exploration of the film's box office success and critiques, we delve into the financial triumphs, audience reception, and the critical assessments that accompanied the cinematic journey of the Grinch.

Box Office Triumph:

Released on November 17, 2000, "How the Grinch Stole Christmas" entered theaters as a highly anticipated holiday release. Boasting the star power of Jim Carrey in the titular role and the imaginative direction of Ron Howard, the film had all the ingredients to draw audiences seeking a festive cinematic experience.

The box office performance of the film exceeded even the most optimistic expectations. "How the Grinch Stole Christmas" secured its place as a holiday blockbuster, grossing over $55 million in its opening weekend in the United States. This impressive debut marked the beginning of a successful theatrical run that would extend well into the holiday season.

As December unfolded, the film continued to dominate the box office, maintaining its strong performance week after week. By the end of its theatrical run, "How the Grinch Stole Christmas" had amassed a staggering worldwide gross of over $345 million, making it one of the highest-grossing holiday films of all time. The financial success of the film not only solidified its place in the annals of box office history but also underscored the enduring appeal of the Grinch's timeless tale during the holiday season.

Factors Contributing to Box Office Success:

Several factors contributed to the exceptional box office success of "How the Grinch Stole Christmas," transforming it into a holiday blockbuster.

1. Jim Carrey's Magnetic Performance:

At the forefront of the film's appeal was the magnetic and transformative performance of Jim Carrey as the Grinch. Carrey's comedic prowess, physicality, and ability to embody the eccentric character of the Grinch became a major selling point. Audiences were drawn to theaters not only for the beloved story but also to witness Carrey's interpretation of the iconic Dr. Seuss character. His dynamic and energetic portrayal added a layer of entertainment that resonated with viewers of all ages.

2. Festive Timing of Release:

The film's release strategy played a crucial role in its box office triumph. Opening in mid-November, "How the Grinch Stole Christmas" strategically positioned itself as the go-to holiday film for families as the festive season commenced. This timing allowed the film to enjoy a sustained theatrical run, capitalizing on the heightened interest in Christmas-themed entertainment during the weeks leading up to the holiday.

3. Nostalgia and Familiarity with the Source Material:

Dr. Seuss's original book, "How the Grinch Stole Christmas," had already achieved iconic status as a beloved holiday classic. The film capitalized on the nostalgia associated with the source material, attracting audiences familiar with the timeless tale. The adaptation aimed to capture the essence of Seuss's whimsical world while expanding on the narrative to create a cinematic experience that would resonate with both fans of the book and new audiences.

4. Universal Themes and Family-Friendly Appeal:

The Grinch's redemption arc and the film's overarching themes of love, compassion, and the true meaning of Christmas contributed to its universal appeal. The narrative's family-friendly nature made it an ideal choice for audiences spanning multiple generations. Families seeking a heartwarming and festive experience found in "How the Grinch Stole Christmas" a film that catered to both children and adults, fostering a sense of togetherness during the holiday season.

Audience Reception:

While the box office numbers reflected widespread success, the audience reception to "How the Grinch Stole Christmas" was equally positive. Viewers embraced the film as a joyous and entertaining addition to their holiday traditions. Families, in particular, found in the film a shared experience that encapsulated the magic of Christmas.

1. Multigenerational Appeal:

One of the film's notable achievements was its ability to appeal to audiences of all ages. Children were captivated by the whimsical world of Whoville, the endearing characters, and the

Grinch's comedic antics. Meanwhile, adults appreciated the nostalgic elements, the film's humor, and the underlying messages about kindness and redemption. "How the Grinch Stole Christmas" successfully bridged generational gaps, becoming a film that families could enjoy together.

2. Festive Atmosphere and Holiday Spirit:

Audiences praised the film for its ability to capture the festive atmosphere of Christmas. The visual spectacle of Whoville's decorations, the joyous celebrations, and the film's overall commitment to creating a holiday ambiance resonated with viewers. For many, watching "How the Grinch Stole Christmas" became a cherished tradition that signaled the official start of the holiday season.

3. Jim Carrey's Transformative Performance:

Jim Carrey's portrayal of the Grinch received widespread acclaim for its comedic brilliance and commitment to the character. Carrey's ability to convey both the humor and underlying humanity of the Grinch added depth to the film. Viewers appreciated the actor's physical comedy, expressive facial contortions, and his ability to bring a beloved character to life in a way that felt both faithful to the source material and uniquely his own.

4. Emotional Resonance and Heartfelt Moments:

Beneath the film's comedic exterior, audiences discovered moments of genuine emotion and heartfelt storytelling. The redemption arc of the Grinch, Cindy Lou Who's unwavering belief in goodness, and the film's messages about love and generosity resonated on an emotional level.

Viewers found themselves laughing at the Grinch's antics one moment and wiping away tears during poignant scenes the next, creating a well-rounded and emotionally satisfying viewing experience.

Critical Assessments:

While audience reception was overwhelmingly positive, critical assessments of "How the Grinch Stole Christmas" varied. Critics engaged in discussions about the film's merits, its deviations from the source material, and the balance between humor and sentimentality.

1. Deviations from Dr. Seuss's Source Material:

One common point of discussion among critics was the film's deviations from Dr. Seuss's original book. While the source material was relatively brief, the film expanded on the narrative, introducing new characters, subplots, and comedic elements. Some critics appreciated these additions as necessary for a feature-length adaptation, while others argued that the film strayed too far from the simplicity of Seuss's storytelling.

2. Tone and Balance of Humor:

The film's tone, balancing humor with sentimentality, sparked debates among critics. While many praised the film for successfully infusing humor into the narrative, others felt that certain comedic elements, particularly Jim Carrey's physical comedy, bordered on being overly exaggerated. The question of whether the film struck the right balance between maintaining the humor of the original tale and introducing new comedic elements became a point of contention.

3. Length and Pacing:

Some critics raised concerns about the film's pacing, citing its feature-length runtime as a potential drawback. Dr. Seuss's original book, being a short story, presented a challenge in terms of expanding the narrative without compromising its essence. While the film aimed to provide a more comprehensive exploration of the Grinch's world, a few critics felt that certain scenes could have been streamlined for a more concise viewing experience.

4. Visual Aesthetics and Production Design:

The visual aesthetics of Whoville and the overall production design faced both praise and critique. Some critics commended the film's commitment to bringing Seussian whimsy to life, applauding the vibrant colors and imaginative sets. However, a minority felt that the exaggerated and unconventional design choices bordered on being too fantastical, creating a visual style that might not resonate with all viewers.

Legacy and Continued Impact:

Despite the varied critical assessments, "How the Grinch Stole Christmas" has left an indelible mark on the landscape of holiday cinema. Its box office success, coupled with positive audience reception, has solidified its status as a perennial favorite. The film's legacy extends beyond its initial release, with each holiday season bringing renewed interest and viewership.

1. Annual Holiday Tradition:

For many families, watching "How the Grinch Stole Christmas" has become an annual holiday tradition. The film's availability on various streaming platforms, coupled with its regular television broadcasts during the holiday season, ensures that it remains a staple in households around the world. The Grinch's antics and the heartwarming messages of the film continue to resonate with viewers, creating a sense of nostalgia and festive joy.

2. Cultural Impact and Merchandising:

The Grinch, as portrayed by Jim Carrey, has become an enduring cultural icon. The character's distinctive appearance, catchphrases, and comedic moments have been embraced beyond the confines of the film. The Grinch's face adorns merchandise, from holiday-themed clothing to ornaments, further solidifying his status as a symbol of Christmas.

3. Continued Viewership Across Generations:

The film's ability to attract new generations of viewers speaks to its timeless appeal. Children who first experienced the Grinch's holiday misadventures in the early 2000s now share the film with their own children, creating a multigenerational connection to the narrative. The enduring popularity of "How the Grinch Stole Christmas" transcends generational boundaries, making it a film that continues to be passed down as a cherished part of holiday celebrations.

Conclusion:

In the realm of holiday cinema, "How the Grinch Stole Christmas" stands as a testament to the enduring magic of Dr. Seuss's timeless tale. Its box office triumph, positive audience reception, and lasting impact on holiday traditions underscore the film's significance in the pantheon of festive classics. While critical assessments may vary, the Grinch's journey from a misunderstood recluse to a symbol of redemption and generosity continues to captivate audiences each December. As the film's legacy endures, "How the Grinch Stole Christmas" remains a shining example of the power of storytelling to bring joy, laughter, and the true spirit of Christmas to audiences around the world.

In the realm of contemporary Christmas classics, "Elf" stands as a delightful and whimsical addition to the holiday film canon. Directed by Jon Favreau and starring Will Ferrell as the endearing Buddy the Elf, the film brings a unique flavor to the Christmas genre through its inventive use of the fish-out-of-water comedy trope. In this exploration of "Elf" and its fish-out-of-water elements, we delve into the charm, humor, and narrative significance that arise as Buddy, a human raised by elves at the North Pole, navigates the bustling and cynical world of New York City.

Introduction to Buddy the Elf:

The fish-out-of-water comedy in "Elf" is anchored in the character of Buddy, played with exuberance and childlike wonder by Will Ferrell. The film opens with a unique premise: Buddy is a human who accidentally crawls into Santa's gift sack as a baby and is unwittingly transported to the North Pole. Raised by elves, Buddy grows up believing himself to be one of Santa's workshop denizens until he discovers the truth about his human origins.

Buddy's introduction to the audience is marked by his sheer enthusiasm for all things Christmas. The humor emerges from the stark contrast between Buddy's childlike innocence and the more pragmatic and jaded world he is about to encounter. As Buddy embarks on his journey to New York City to find his biological father, the stage is set for a fish-out-of-water comedy that combines heartwarming moments with laugh-out-loud humor.

Cultural Clashes and Christmas Cheer:

The fish-out-of-water dynamic in "Elf" is fueled by the stark cultural clashes between Buddy's fantastical upbringing in the North Pole and the bustling, mundane reality of New York City. From his first steps into the city, Buddy's wide-eyed wonder at everything—from revolving doors to escalators—serves as a comedic device that plays on the audience's familiarity with urban life.

The film cleverly juxtaposes Buddy's unbridled Christmas cheer with the indifference and skepticism of New Yorkers. His penchant for spreading holiday joy, bursting into spontaneous caroling, and his genuine belief in the magic of Christmas create humorous situations and misunderstandings. The clash between Buddy's infectious enthusiasm and the more cynical attitudes of those around him becomes a recurring source of comedy throughout the film.

Navigating Relationships:

One of the central themes in the fish-out-of-water narrative of "Elf" is Buddy's attempt to navigate relationships in a world where he doesn't quite fit in. His earnest efforts to connect with his biological father, Walter Hobbs (played by James Caan), provide both comedic and poignant moments. Walter, a workaholic with little time for holiday cheer, is initially bewildered and frustrated by Buddy's presence.

The humor arises from Buddy's relentless attempts to bond with Walter, often leading to awkward and humorous situations. Whether it's Buddy decorating Walter's office with handmade Christmas decorations or his unfiltered expressions of affection, the film mines these interactions for both laughs and heartfelt moments. The juxtaposition of Buddy's childlike innocence with Walter's stern demeanor creates a dynamic that underscores the transformative power of holiday spirit.

Buddy's interactions with his half-brother Michael (played by Daniel Tay) and his attempts at wooing Jovie (played by Zooey Deschanel) further contribute to the fish-out-of-water comedy. His naivety and unconventional approaches to relationships result in a series of humorous and endearing moments, reinforcing the film's overarching theme of the impact of genuine Christmas spirit on the lives of those around Buddy.

Navigating the Workplace:

The workplace becomes another arena for fish-out-of-water comedy as Buddy secures a job at the Greenway Press, the company where Walter works. The contrast between Buddy's elfin approach to work—gleefully answering phones by cheerfully announcing, "Buddy the Elf, what's your favorite color?"—and the corporate environment of the publishing company sets the stage for comedic misunderstandings and clashes.

Buddy's innocence clashes with the office culture, leading to humorous moments such as his impromptu participation in a mailroom snowball fight and his attempts to spread holiday cheer in a workplace more accustomed to stress and deadlines. The workplace dynamic becomes a microcosm of the broader fish-out-of-water theme, highlighting the absurdity of Buddy's elfin antics in the context of a modern urban setting.

Cinematic Techniques and Visual Humor:

The fish-out-of-water comedy in "Elf" is not solely reliant on dialogue; it is amplified through Jon Favreau's adept use of cinematic techniques and visual humor. The film employs sight gags, physical comedy, and visual juxtapositions to accentuate the comedic contrast between Buddy's whimsical world and the reality of New York City.

1. Forced Perspective and Size Discrepancies:

A notable visual element contributing to the fish-out-of-water humor is the use of forced perspective to emphasize Buddy's size in relation to the elves and, later, to the regular-sized humans in New York. Scenes in the North Pole workshop showcase Buddy towering over his elf companions, emphasizing the fantastical nature of his upbringing. As Buddy navigates New York City, the same technique is used to highlight his otherness, creating a visual spectacle that elicits laughter.

2. Costuming and Visual Contrasts:

The film's costuming choices play a role in reinforcing the fish-out-of-water dynamic. Buddy's distinctive elf costume, complete with vibrant green tights and a pointy hat, stands out against the more muted and conventional attire of the New Yorkers. The visual contrast between Buddy's whimsical wardrobe and the attire of those around him becomes a source of both humor and commentary on societal norms.

3. Set Design and Iconic Locations:

The film's set design contributes to the comedic atmosphere by creating iconic locations that emphasize Buddy's unconventional presence. Whether it's the elaborately decorated North Pole workshop or the stark, corporate setting of Walter's office, the visual elements enhance the fish-out-of-water narrative. The film strategically uses recognizable New York City landmarks, such as the Empire State Building and Rockefeller Center, as backdrops for Buddy's escapades, adding to the humor and charm of his journey.

Narrative Significance:

Beyond its comedic elements, the fish-out-of-water theme in "Elf" serves a narrative purpose that goes beyond surface-level humor. Buddy's unique perspective and unwavering commitment to the Christmas spirit challenge the status quo and inspire those around him to rediscover the joy and wonder of the holiday season.

1. Transformative Impact on Characters:

The fish-out-of-water dynamic becomes a catalyst for transformative arcs among the characters Buddy encounters. Walter, initially dismissive of Buddy's whimsy, undergoes a gradual change as he reconnects with the joy of Christmas and the importance of family. Michael, Buddy's half-brother, experiences a rekindling of childhood wonder through his interactions with his festive sibling.

2. Resilience of Christmas Spirit:

The film's fish-out-of-water theme reinforces the resilience of the Christmas spirit in the face of skepticism and cynicism. Buddy's unyielding commitment to spreading joy becomes a contagious force that challenges the jaded perspectives of those he encounters. The narrative suggests that the magic of Christmas is not confined to the North Pole but can thrive even in the most unlikely of places.

3. Blending Heart and Humor:

The fish-out-of-water comedy in "Elf" seamlessly blends heart and humor. While the film elicits laughter through Buddy's misadventures and cultural clashes, it also invites audiences to reflect on the transformative power of embracing childlike wonder and the true spirit of Christmas. The narrative significance of the fish-out-of-water theme lies in its ability to convey a timeless message about the importance of joy, love, and togetherness during the holiday season.

Conclusion:

"Elf" stands as a testament to the enduring appeal of fish-out-of-water comedy when infused with heart, charm, and a touch of Christmas magic. Buddy the Elf's journey from the North Pole to the streets of New York City captivates audiences with its humor, visual spectacle, and poignant moments. The film's fish-out-of-water elements contribute to its status as a modern holiday classic, reminding viewers that, even in the midst of the ordinary, the extraordinary joy of Christmas can be found when seen through the eyes of an elf. Through laughter, warmth, and a sprinkle of holiday enchantment, "Elf" continues to weave its spell, inviting audiences into a world where fish-out-of-water comedy and the spirit of Christmas coalesce in a celebration of the extraordinary in the everyday.

Whimsical Filmmaking Style

In the kaleidoscope of holiday cinema, "Elf" emerges as a beacon of whimsy, enchantment, and unbridled joy. Directed by Jon Favreau and starring Will Ferrell as the lovable and larger-than-life Buddy the Elf, the film not only captivates audiences with its heartwarming narrative but also distinguishes itself through its whimsical filmmaking style. This exploration delves into the elements that contribute to the film's whimsical charm, from visual aesthetics and set design to music and comedic timing.

Introduction to Whimsy:

"Elf" unfolds as a modern fairy tale, and its whimsical filmmaking style serves as the enchanting brushstroke that brings this magical narrative to life. From the moment Buddy the Elf takes his first steps into the bustling world of New York City, the film immerses viewers in a visual and auditory symphony of whimsy. This stylistic choice not only enhances the comedic elements but also underscores the film's overarching message of embracing the extraordinary in the ordinary.

Visual Aesthetics:

The visual aesthetics of "Elf" play a pivotal role in establishing its whimsical tone. The film's color palette is a vibrant tapestry of holiday hues, with the festive reds and greens of Buddy's elf costume juxtaposed against the wintry whites and grays of the North Pole and New York City. This deliberate use of color heightens the visual contrast between

Buddy's fantastical world and the reality he encounters, creating a sense of visual delight.

The set design further contributes to the film's whimsical atmosphere. The North Pole workshop, with its candy-cane striped poles, oversized gift-wrapping stations, and Santa's towering throne, is a whimsical wonderland brought to life. The decision to embrace exaggerated and fantastical set elements serves not only to transport viewers into a fairy-tale realm but also to accentuate the fish-out-of-water comedy as Buddy navigates through environments that are a stark departure from the North Pole.

New York City itself becomes a canvas for whimsy, transformed into a holiday spectacle through the lens of the film. Landmarks such as Rockefeller Center, Central Park, and the Empire State Building are adorned with festive decorations, creating a visually enchanting backdrop for Buddy's adventures. The juxtaposition of everyday locations transformed into magical settings reinforces the film's theme of finding magic in the ordinary.

Costuming and Character Design:

The whimsical nature of "Elf" is embodied in the costuming and character design choices. Buddy's elf costume, with its pointy hat, jingle bells, and vibrant green tights, becomes an iconic visual representation of the character's childlike innocence and festive spirit. The costume not only serves as a comedic element but also symbolizes Buddy's unwavering commitment to his elfin identity.

In contrast to Buddy's elf attire, the costumes of other characters, particularly those in the corporate setting of Greenway Press, highlight the visual disparity between Buddy's whimsical world and the more conventional surroundings. This visual contrast becomes a source of humor and commentary on societal norms, emphasizing Buddy's departure from the ordinary.

Beyond Buddy, the character design extends to the elves of the North Pole, each with their distinctive looks and personalities. The film embraces diversity in elfin appearances, from the towering Ming Ming to the tech-savvy Eugene. These character design choices contribute to the overall whimsy of the North Pole community, creating a visually rich and diverse ensemble that adds depth to the film's fantastical elements.

Cinematography and Forced Perspective:

The whimsical filmmaking style of "Elf" is further accentuated by Jon Favreau's adept use of cinematography, including the strategic application of forced perspective. This technique is employed to highlight Buddy's size in relation to the elves and, later, to the regular-sized humans in New York. Scenes in the North Pole workshop showcase Buddy towering over his elf companions, creating a visually striking and humorous spectacle.

The forced perspective is not merely a visual trick but a narrative device that reinforces the fish-out-of-water comedy. The exaggerated size discrepancies underscore Buddy's otherness and emphasize the fantastical nature of his upbringing. The strategic use of forced perspective adds a layer of visual complexity to the film's comedic moments and enhances the overall whimsy of the narrative.

Musical Score and Soundtrack:

The whimsy of "Elf" extends beyond its visual elements to the auditory realm, with a musical score and soundtrack that amplify the film's enchanting atmosphere. Composed by John Debney, the score combines orchestral arrangements with playful melodies, creating a musical tapestry that mirrors the film's emotional beats and comedic timing.

The score incorporates elements of holiday music, infusing the film with festive cheer. Familiar tunes are reimagined to complement the whimsical narrative, adding a layer of recognition for audiences. Whether it's the joyful refrains of "Santa Claus Is Coming to Town" or the playful motifs accompanying Buddy's misadventures, the musical score becomes an integral part of the film's whimsical identity.

In addition to the original score, "Elf" features a soundtrack that includes classic holiday songs, further contributing to the film's festive ambiance. These songs, carefully selected to complement key moments in the narrative, enhance the whimsical experience for viewers. The marriage of visual whimsy with a musical backdrop creates a sensory journey that envelops audiences in the magic of Buddy's world.

Comedic Timing and Performances:

At the heart of "Elf's" whimsical charm is its comedic timing, brought to life through the performances of the cast, particularly Will Ferrell as Buddy the Elf. Ferrell's portrayal is characterized by an exuberant physicality and a childlike sincerity that infuses the character with infectious energy. His comedic timing, whether in delivering lines with unwavering enthusiasm or engaging in physical comedy, contributes to the film's whimsical humor.

The supporting cast, including James Caan as Walter Hobbs, Zooey Deschanel as Jovie, and Bob Newhart as Papa Elf, further enhances the film's comedic dynamics. Each actor embraces the whimsical nature of their characters, delivering performances that blend humor with heart. The interactions between Buddy and the various characters, from the elves at the North Pole to the denizens of New York City, are orchestrated with a keen understanding of comedic timing, creating a tapestry of laughter woven into the narrative.

The film's script, penned by David Berenbaum, incorporates witty dialogue and humorous situations that align with the whimsical tone. The comedic elements are not solely reliant on verbal exchanges but extend to physical comedy, sight gags, and situational humor. The film's ability to seamlessly blend different forms of comedy contributes to its whimsical and lighthearted atmosphere.

Narrative Whimsy and Emotional Resonance:

While "Elf" is undeniably a comedy, its whimsical filmmaking style goes beyond generating laughs; it cultivates emotional resonance. The film's ability to balance humor with moments of genuine warmth and sincerity elevates it from being a mere comedy to a heartfelt exploration of the transformative power of Christmas spirit.

The narrative whimsy is reflected in Buddy's unwavering belief in the magic of Christmas and his infectious enthusiasm. As he navigates through a world that often questions or dismisses his elfin identity, the film invites audiences to suspend disbelief and embrace the fantastical elements. This narrative whimsy becomes a conduit for conveying timeless messages about love, family, and the enduring joy of the holiday season.

The emotional resonance is particularly evident in scenes that highlight Buddy's impact on those around him. Whether it's the transformative effect on his cynical father, the rekindling of holiday spirit in his half-brother, or the blossoming romance with Jovie, the film weaves moments of genuine emotion into its whimsical tapestry. The ability to evoke laughter and tears in equal measure contributes to the film's enduring popularity and its status as a contemporary holiday classic.

Conclusion:

"Elf" stands as a testament to the enchanting possibilities of whimsical filmmaking. From its visual aesthetics and set design to its musical score and comedic performances, the film creates a world where the ordinary becomes extraordinary, and the joy of the holiday season is celebrated with unbridled enthusiasm. The whimsical elements not only contribute to the film's comedic charm but also serve as a vehicle for delivering timeless messages about the magic of Christmas and the transformative power of embracing childlike wonder. As audiences revisit Buddy's journey each holiday season, they are invited into a realm where whimsy and heart coalesce, reminding us all to find joy in the fantastical, the magical, and the whimsically extraordinary moments that define the true spirit of Christmas.

In the tapestry of holiday cinema, "Elf" emerges as a vibrant thread, weaving together themes that transcend comedy to embrace the true spirit of the season. Directed by Jon Favreau and starring Will Ferrell as the exuberant Buddy the Elf, the film not only elicits laughter but also serves as a heartwarming celebration of themes promoting holiday cheer. This exploration delves into the thematic elements that contribute to the film's enduring appeal, from the importance of childlike wonder to the transformative power of love, family, and the magic of Christmas.

Childlike Wonder and Unwavering Belief:

At the heart of "Elf" beats the pulse of childlike wonder, embodied in the character of Buddy. Raised by elves at the North Pole, Buddy's perspective on the world is shaped by the enchantment of Christmas and the magical traditions of Santa's workshop. His unwavering belief in the spirit of the season becomes a guiding light that permeates every aspect of the film.

Buddy's childlike wonder is infectious, creating a ripple effect that touches everyone he encounters. From his first steps into New York City, where the ordinary becomes extraordinary through his eyes, to his interactions with his newfound family, Buddy's perspective challenges the cynicism and skepticism prevalent in the adult world. The film suggests that, by embracing childlike wonder, individuals can rediscover the joy, magic, and possibilities inherent in the holiday season.

The theme of childlike wonder is reflected in various elements of the film's narrative, including Buddy's spontaneous bursts into song, his delight at mundane aspects of city life, and his unbridled enthusiasm for Christmas traditions. These moments serve as a reminder that, in the midst of adult responsibilities and challenges, there exists a reservoir of joy and wonder waiting to be tapped into—a sentiment that resonates profoundly during the holiday season.

Transformative Power of Christmas Spirit:

"Elf" weaves a narrative that underscores the transformative power of Christmas spirit. As Buddy embarks on his journey to reconnect with his biological father, Walter Hobbs, and navigate the complexities of the human world, his commitment to spreading joy becomes a catalyst for change in the lives of those around him.

The film portrays Christmas spirit not as a passive observance of traditions but as an active force that has the capacity to thaw even the coldest of hearts. Walter Hobbs, initially portrayed as a workaholic with little time for holiday cheer, undergoes a gradual transformation influenced by Buddy's infectious enthusiasm. The film suggests that the magic of Christmas lies not only in festive decorations and presents but in the ability to connect with others and experience moments of genuine warmth and kindness.

The transformative power of Christmas spirit is not limited to familial relationships. Buddy's interactions with his half-brother Michael, his workplace at Greenway Press, and even the hardened character of Gimbels' manager, played by Faizon Love, reveal the far-reaching impact of genuine joy and generosity. The film invites audiences to consider the potential for positive change that exists within the collective embrace of the holiday spirit.

Family and Belonging:

A central theme in "Elf" is the exploration of family and belonging. As Buddy embarks on a quest to find his biological father, the film navigates the complexities of familial relationships with humor, warmth, and sincerity. The notion of what constitutes a family is expanded beyond biological ties to encompass those who offer love, acceptance, and support.

The juxtaposition of Buddy's elfin identity with his newfound family in New York creates both comedic and poignant moments. Walter's initial disbelief and frustration at Buddy's claims gradually give way to a deeper understanding of the importance of familial bonds. Michael, Buddy's half-brother, experiences a rekindling of sibling connection and discovers the joy of embracing the extraordinary alongside the ordinary.

The North Pole community, with its diverse and quirky characters, serves as an extended family for Buddy. Papa Elf, played by Bob Newhart, becomes a father figure who imparts wisdom and guidance, while the camaraderie among the elves reinforces the theme of family beyond blood relations. The film suggests that family is not solely defined by genetics but by shared experiences, love, and the willingness to embrace one another's uniqueness.

Romance and Joyful Connections:

"Elf" incorporates a delightful romantic subplot between Buddy and Jovie, a department store employee played by Zooey

Deschanel. Their burgeoning romance is characterized by a blend of innocence, humor, and the shared joy of the holiday season. The film explores the idea that love can blossom in unexpected places and that genuine connections are nurtured through shared laughter, kindness, and a mutual appreciation for the magic of Christmas.

The romance between Buddy and Jovie is a testament to the film's ability to balance humor with heartfelt moments. Buddy's earnest attempts at wooing Jovie, from serenading her with Christmas carols to transforming the department store into a winter wonderland, contribute to the film's overall theme of spreading joy and finding love in the most unlikely of circumstances.

Beyond the central romance, "Elf" portrays joyful connections between characters that transcend romantic relationships. Buddy's interactions with his coworkers at Greenway Press, the residents of New York City, and even the inhabitants of the North Pole highlight the joy that can be found in shared laughter, camaraderie, and the simple pleasures of human connection.

Navigating Challenges with Positivity:

"Elf" embraces the theme of navigating challenges with positivity and resilience. Buddy's journey is marked by numerous obstacles, from the initial disbelief of those around him to the complexities of adapting to the human world. However, his approach to challenges is characterized by unwavering optimism, a refusal to succumb to negativity, and a commitment to finding solutions with a smile.

The film suggests that positivity and a joyful outlook have the power to overcome even the most daunting of challenges. Whether it's Buddy's determination to bring holiday cheer to a cynical workplace or his ability to transform a dingy apartment into a festive haven, the character exemplifies the idea that a positive attitude can be a catalyst for change.

Buddy's resilience in the face of adversity becomes a source of inspiration for those around him. His ability to navigate challenges with childlike optimism encourages others to reevaluate their perspectives and embrace the potential for joy, even in the midst of difficulties. This thematic element reinforces the notion that, during the holiday season and beyond, a positive mindset can be a transformative force.

Balancing Tradition and Innovation:

"Elf" navigates the theme of balancing tradition and innovation, particularly in its portrayal of Christmas customs. While Buddy embodies the traditional spirit of Christmas through his love for caroling, decorating, and spreading joy, the film also acknowledges the need for adaptation and flexibility in embracing new traditions.

The clash between Buddy's elfin customs and the pragmatic realities of the human world becomes a source of humor, but it also prompts reflection on the evolving nature of holiday traditions. The film suggests that, while certain customs may change or encounter resistance, the core values of love, kindness, and togetherness remain timeless.

The juxtaposition of traditional Christmas elements, such as the North Pole workshop and caroling, with modern interpretations, including a chaotic snowball fight in the mailroom and a quirky rendition of "Santa Claus Is Coming to Town," creates a thematic balance that celebrates both the nostalgic and the contemporary aspects of the holiday season.

Festive Atmosphere and Community Engagement:

"Elf" fosters a festive atmosphere that extends beyond the screen to engage audiences in the celebration of holiday cheer. The film's visual aesthetics, musical score, and comedic elements combine to create a sensory experience that invites viewers to immerse themselves in the magic of Christmas.

The community engagement theme is exemplified by Buddy's interactions with the denizens of New York City. From his impromptu participation in a mailroom snowball fight to his efforts to spread holiday cheer at Greenway Press, Buddy becomes a catalyst for transforming ordinary spaces into festive havens. The film suggests that the collective engagement of individuals in spreading joy can create a ripple effect that transcends individual actions.

The department store setting, particularly Gimbels, becomes a microcosm of community engagement, as Buddy's influence transforms the workplace into a hub of holiday spirit. The joyous atmosphere permeates the film, encouraging audiences to consider the impact of their own contributions to fostering a sense of community and festive celebration during the holiday season.

Conclusion:

"Elf" stands as a cinematic celebration of themes promoting holiday cheer, encapsulating the magic, warmth, and transformative power of Christmas spirit. From the importance of childlike wonder and unwavering belief to the exploration of family, love, and positive resilience, the film invites audiences into a world where laughter and heartfelt moments coalesce in a joyful tapestry.

As viewers revisit Buddy's journey each holiday season, they are not merely entertained by the comedic escapades but reminded of the enduring values that define the true spirit of Christmas. "Elf" becomes more than a film; it becomes a festive companion that encourages audiences to embrace childlike wonder, navigate challenges with positivity, and foster connections that celebrate the joy, love, and magic of the holiday season. In its thematic richness, "Elf" invites us all to rediscover the extraordinary in the ordinary, embodying the essence of holiday cheer that resonates far beyond the confines of the screen.

In the realm of holiday cinema, "Elf" has not only earned its place as a contemporary classic but has left an indelible mark on popular culture. Directed by Jon Favreau and starring Will Ferrell as the lovable Buddy the Elf, the film's lasting cultural impact extends far beyond the boundaries of the screen. This exploration delves into the factors that have contributed to the enduring popularity of "Elf," examining its influence on holiday traditions, its status as a quotable cultural phenomenon, and its resonance in the digital age.

Holiday Tradition Reinvented:

"Elf" stands as a cinematic reinvention of holiday tradition, infusing the familiar elements of Christmas with a modern, comedic twist. The film's narrative, centered around Buddy's journey from the North Pole to New York City, reimagines traditional Christmas themes and characters, presenting them through the lens of humor, whimsy, and heartwarming charm.

One of the key elements that has contributed to the lasting cultural impact of "Elf" is its ability to become a staple in holiday viewing traditions. Families and friends across generations have embraced the film as an essential part of their annual celebrations. Whether it's gathering around the television to watch Buddy's adventures or quoting iconic lines from the movie, "Elf" has become synonymous with the festive season.

The film's portrayal of holiday traditions, from the decorating of trees and singing of carols to the exchange of gifts, has resonated with audiences as a reflection of their own festive customs. However, "Elf" does more than merely depict these traditions; it reinvigorates them with a sense of joy, humor, and a reminder of the importance of embracing childlike wonder during the holiday season.

Quotable Cultural Phenomenon:

"Elf" has transcended its status as a film to become a quotable cultural phenomenon, with lines from the movie woven into everyday discourse and holiday banter. The script, penned by David Berenbaum, is a treasure trove of memorable and humorous lines that have become ingrained in the lexicon of holiday enthusiasts.

Buddy's enthusiastic exclamations, such as "Santa! I know him!" and "I just like to smile; smiling's my favorite," have become iconic expressions of holiday cheer. The film's witty dialogue, delivered with comedic timing by the cast, has resulted in a plethora of quotes that resonate not only during the holiday season but throughout the year.

Beyond Buddy's lines, "Elf" has spawned a collection of memorable quotes that capture the film's humor, warmth, and irreverent take on holiday traditions. Whether it's Walter Hobbs's exasperated "Buddy, I have to go to work," or Jovie's deadpan "Buddy, the world's best cup of coffee," these lines have become part of the cultural tapestry, invoked in conversations, social media posts, and even holiday decorations.

The film's quotability has facilitated its integration into various forms of media and entertainment. From memes and

GIFs shared online to references in television shows and other films, "Elf" has permeated popular culture as a source of humor and relatable moments, further cementing its status as a quotable cultural phenomenon.

Digital Age Resonance:

"Elf" has demonstrated a remarkable resonance in the digital age, leveraging online platforms and social media to extend its cultural influence. The film's popularity has been propelled by a digital ecosystem that allows fans to share their favorite moments, quotes, and experiences in real-time, creating a sense of community among viewers.

Social media platforms, particularly during the holiday season, witness a surge in references to "Elf." Hashtags such as #BuddyTheElf and #ElfQuotes trend as users share their favorite scenes, quotes, and memes. The film's digital presence extends beyond official promotional efforts to grassroots movements driven by fans who embrace "Elf" as an integral part of their online holiday celebrations.

The film's influence is not confined to the holiday season, as references to "Elf" permeate discussions on comedy, pop culture, and the enduring appeal of classic films. The digital age has provided a platform for fans to express their love for "Elf" through creative content, including fan art, parody videos, and digital collages that celebrate the film's humor and heart.

"Elf" has also found a second life on streaming platforms, allowing new generations of viewers to discover and embrace the film. The accessibility of the movie on digital platforms has ensured that it remains a relevant and beloved part of the holiday viewing landscape, transcending the confines of traditional broadcast schedules.

Merchandising and Brand Collaborations:

The cultural impact of "Elf" is further evident in the extensive merchandising and brand collaborations that have emerged around the film. From festive sweaters featuring Buddy's iconic face to holiday-themed merchandise, "Elf" has become a marketable brand that extends beyond the screen.

The film's characters, especially Buddy the Elf, have been featured in a wide range of merchandise, including toys, ornaments, and collectibles. The visual elements of the film, such as Buddy's distinctive elf costume and the vibrant color palette, have translated seamlessly into products that capitalize on the film's festive and whimsical aesthetic.

Brand collaborations have embraced the cultural phenomenon of "Elf" to create limited-edition items and experiences. From themed food products, such as Buddy-inspired cereal and candy, to holiday-themed events and activations, the film's influence has extended into the realms of retail and experiential marketing.

"Elf" has also become a prominent figure in holiday-themed advertising campaigns. Brands leverage the film's recognizable characters and quotes to create festive and memorable advertisements that resonate with audiences during the holiday season. The integration of "Elf" into marketing strategies further cements its status as a cultural touchstone with widespread appeal.

Impact on Holiday Programming:

"Elf" has had a transformative impact on holiday programming, influencing the way networks and streaming platforms curate their seasonal content. The film's popularity has elevated it to a position of prominence in holiday lineups, with frequent broadcasts and dedicated marathons during the festive season.

The demand for "Elf" as a holiday staple has led to strategic programming decisions by networks and streaming services. The film's inclusion in holiday movie marathons, countdowns, and themed programming blocks has become a tradition in itself, signaling its cultural significance in the landscape of seasonal entertainment.

The enduring appeal of "Elf" has also influenced the programming choices of theaters and cinemas during the holiday season. The film's return to the big screen for special screenings and anniversary celebrations reflects its status as a cinematic experience that transcends the home-viewing environment.

Legacy with Future Generations:

"Elf" has secured a lasting legacy with future generations, establishing itself as a film that resonates across age groups and continues to be embraced by new audiences. The film's timeless themes, universal humor, and heartwarming narrative ensure its relevance as a holiday classic that can be passed down from one generation to the next.

The cultural impact of "Elf" is evident in its ability to capture the imaginations of children and adults alike. Buddy the Elf, with his infectious enthusiasm and endearing innocence, has become an iconic character with cross-generational appeal. Parents who grew up watching "Elf" are now introducing the film to their own children, creating a shared experience that reinforces its status as a family tradition.

The film's themes of joy, love, and the magic of Christmas resonate with each new wave of viewers, ensuring that "Elf" remains a relevant and cherished part of the holiday season. The potential for the film's legacy to endure for decades to come is reflected in its continued popularity, cultural relevance, and its ability to evoke laughter and warmth in the hearts of those who revisit Buddy's adventures year after year.

Conclusion:

"Elf" stands as a cinematic phenomenon that has left an indelible mark on popular culture, transcending the boundaries of traditional holiday cinema to become a cultural touchstone. Its lasting cultural impact is characterized by its role in redefining holiday traditions, its status as a quotable phenomenon, its resonance in the digital age, and its influence on merchandising, brand collaborations, and holiday programming.

As audiences continue to embrace the film during the holiday season and beyond, "Elf" solidifies its place as a timeless classic with a legacy that extends far beyond its initial release. The film's enduring popularity with future generations ensures that Buddy the Elf and his festive escapades will

continue to spread joy, laughter, and the true spirit of
Christmas for years to come.

"A Christmas Story" is a cinematic journey through time, immersing audiences in the nostalgic charm of a bygone era. Directed by Bob Clark and based on the semi-autobiographical stories of Jean Shepherd, the film captures the essence of mid-20th-century America, offering a window into the period-specific details that define its narrative landscape. This exploration delves into the meticulous craftsmanship behind the film's recreation of the 1940s and the enduring appeal of its period-specific elements.

Setting the Stage:

The narrative unfolds in Hohman, Indiana, a fictionalized version of Shepherd's hometown of Hammond. The choice of a small, middle-class town in the American Midwest becomes a pivotal element in establishing the period-specific details of the film. The year is 1940, a time marked by post-Depression recovery and the looming shadows of World War II. The decision to anchor the story in this particular era serves as a deliberate choice by the filmmakers to evoke a sense of nostalgia and transport viewers to a simpler time.

1940s Americana:

"A Christmas Story" is a tapestry of 1940s Americana, meticulously crafted to capture the visual, cultural, and societal nuances of the era. The film's production design, costumes, and set decorations pay homage to the iconic imagery associated with mid-20th-century America. From the snowy streets lined with glowing Christmas lights to the interiors adorned with period-appropriate furnishings, every frame is infused with the warmth and authenticity of a Norman Rockwell painting.

The exterior shots of the Parker family home, with its snow-covered roof and picket fence, encapsulate the idyllic suburban setting of 1940s America. The attention to detail extends to the props, such as the classic Red Ryder BB Gun and the Oldsmobile coupe parked in the driveway. These elements contribute to the film's immersive quality, inviting viewers to step into a world where the simplicity of life and the magic of Christmas intersect.

Holiday Traditions:

Central to the film's period-specific details are the holiday traditions that define the Parker family's Christmas celebrations. The meticulously decorated Christmas tree, adorned with tinsel and colorful ornaments, becomes a symbol of festive cheer. The carefully wrapped presents, the anticipation of Christmas morning, and the family's participation in time-honored customs such as caroling and attending church services contribute to the authenticity of the film's portrayal of holiday traditions in the 1940s.

The film captures the essence of a time when holiday festivities were characterized by simplicity and heartfelt joy. The absence of modern-day technological distractions highlights the importance of family togetherness and the shared experiences that define the holiday season. From the careful preparation of the Christmas turkey to the excitement of opening presents by the fireplace, "A Christmas Story" weaves a narrative that harkens back to an era when the magic of

Christmas was found in the genuine connections forged with loved ones.

School Days and Childhood Adventures:

The portrayal of school life and childhood adventures in "A Christmas Story" is steeped in period-specific details that evoke a sense of nostalgia for a bygone era of innocence. The scenes set at Warren G. Harding Elementary School showcase the vintage classrooms, chalkboards, and the camaraderie among classmates. The fashion choices, including the students' clothing and the iconic leg lamp featured in a window display, offer a snapshot of 1940s school culture.

Ralphie Parker's day-to-day life, punctuated by schoolyard escapades and his quest for the coveted Red Ryder BB Gun, reflects the universal experiences of children in the 1940s. The film captures the essence of a time when the simple act of going to school, navigating friendships, and dreaming of Christmas presents defined the world of a young boy. Through Ralphie's eyes, audiences are transported to an era where the challenges of childhood were met with determination, imagination, and the enduring belief in holiday magic.

Fashion and Style:

The period-specific details extend to the fashion and style showcased in "A Christmas Story." The characters' wardrobes are a reflection of 1940s fashion sensibilities, from the tailored suits worn by Ralphie's father to the knee-high socks and woolen coats donned by the children. The film captures the iconic elements of mid-20th-century attire, including the wide-brimmed hats, suspenders, and Mary Jane shoes that were emblematic of the era.

The fashion choices not only contribute to the film's visual authenticity but also serve as a narrative tool, reinforcing the social and cultural context of the 1940s. The contrast between the bundled-up children facing the winter chill and the adults adorned in formal wear during holiday gatherings creates a visual tapestry that reflects the societal norms and expectations of the time.

The leg lamp, a quirky yet iconic element of the film, also serves as a commentary on fashion and style. The lamp, adorned with a fishnet stocking and high-heeled shoe, becomes a humorous symbol of the changing cultural landscape and the influence of popular media on consumer preferences.

Technological Artifacts:

In addition to visual elements, "A Christmas Story" incorporates period-specific technological artifacts that contribute to the film's immersive quality. The vintage radio, a central fixture in the Parker family home, serves as a source of entertainment and information. The clunky yet charming radios of the 1940s, with their warm tones and analog dials, become a backdrop for scenes that capture the family's interactions and the unfolding narrative of Ralphie's Christmas quest.

The inclusion of the iconic Ovaltine decoder ring, a popular promotional item of the time, further emphasizes the technological artifacts that were emblematic of 1940s consumer culture. The film uses these artifacts not merely as set decorations but as integral components that enrich the storytelling experience and transport viewers to a specific moment in history.

Cultural References and Media:

"A Christmas Story" is interwoven with cultural references and media that define the period-specific details of the narrative. The film seamlessly incorporates elements such as the Little Orphan Annie radio show, a popular program of the era, and the corresponding Ovaltine promotion that captures the excitement of children waiting for a secret message.

The portrayal of the family's visit to the Higbee's department store, complete with its elaborate Christmas displays and Santa Claus meet-and-greet, reflects the consumer culture and retail traditions of 1940s America. The bustling city streets adorned with holiday decorations and the presence of iconic brands evoke a sense of nostalgia for a time when holiday shopping was a communal and festive experience.

The film also introduces the character of Black Bart, the fictional outlaw in Ralphie's imagination. This nod to the cowboy and western genres popular during the 1940s serves as a playful homage to the cultural influences that shaped the fantasies of children during that era.

Conclusion:

In "A Christmas Story," the magic of the holiday season is interwoven with period-specific details that transport audiences to the heart of 1940s America. The film's meticulous attention to setting, traditions, school life, fashion, technology, and cultural references creates a tapestry of nostalgia that resonates with viewers across generations.

As audiences revisit the timeless tale of Ralphie's Christmas quest, they are not merely spectators but participants in a journey through time—a journey that captures the essence of a bygone era and invites us to relive the simplicity, warmth, and enduring charm of 1940s Americana. "A Christmas Story" stands as a testament to the power of period-specific details in shaping a cinematic experience that transcends generations, becoming a cherished part of the holiday traditions for those who yearn for the magic of a simpler time.

"A Christmas Story" is more than a holiday film; it's a cinematic time capsule that captures the essence of childhood nostalgia. Directed by Bob Clark and inspired by Jean Shepherd's semi-autobiographical stories, the film seamlessly weaves a narrative that resonates with audiences on a deeply personal level. This exploration delves into the ways in which "A Christmas Story" connects with childhood nostalgia, tapping into universal experiences, relatable characters, and the timeless themes of growing up during the holiday season.

Universal Coming-of-Age Themes:

At the heart of "A Christmas Story" is the universal theme of coming-of-age, a narrative thread that weaves through the fabric of childhood nostalgia. The film chronicles the adventures of young Ralphie Parker, navigating the challenges and joys of growing up in the small town of Hohman, Indiana. As Ralphie embarks on his quest for the coveted Red Ryder BB Gun, audiences are transported to a time when childhood dreams and desires were simple yet profound.

The film's portrayal of childhood resonates with viewers who recall the excitement, wonder, and anticipation of the holiday season. Whether it's the eager anticipation of Christmas morning, the quest for the perfect present, or the imaginative adventures in the schoolyard, "A Christmas Story" taps into the shared experiences that define the journey from childhood to adolescence.

The character of Ralphie serves as a relatable protagonist, embodying the universal struggles and triumphs of growing up. His day-to-day encounters with bullies, quirky family dynamics, and the quest for parental approval are timeless elements that transcend the specific era depicted in the film. By grounding the narrative in relatable coming-of-age themes, "A Christmas Story" becomes a vessel for audiences to revisit the emotions, challenges, and innocence of their own childhoods.

Quintessential Holiday Traditions:

The film's connection with childhood nostalgia is intricately tied to the quintessential holiday traditions it portrays. From the careful selection of the Christmas tree to the ritualistic opening of presents, "A Christmas Story" captures the essence of timeless customs that define the holiday experience for children. The scenes of the Parker family engaging in these traditions evoke a sense of warmth and familiarity, inviting audiences to reflect on their own holiday memories.

The anticipation of Santa Claus, the festive decorations adorning the home, and the communal experiences such as caroling and school pageants transport viewers back to a time when the magic of Christmas was intertwined with the joy of shared traditions. The film becomes a nostalgic reflection of the holiday season as seen through the eyes of a child, where every moment is infused with a sense of wonder and excitement.

Ralphie's quest for the Red Ryder BB Gun becomes a symbol of childhood yearning, representing the innocent desires and dreams that define the holiday season for young minds. The film's portrayal of these traditions not only serves as a reflection of the past but also prompts audiences to connect with their own cherished memories of holidays spent with family and friends.

Familial Dynamics and Quirks:

One of the enduring strengths of "A Christmas Story" lies in its portrayal of familial dynamics and quirks that resonate with audiences' own experiences. The Parker family, with its distinctive personalities and idiosyncrasies, becomes a microcosm of relatable family life. From the endearing yet exasperating interactions with Ralphie's younger brother Randy to the humorous exchanges between the parents, the film captures the nuances of family relationships with humor and authenticity.

The Old Man, portrayed by Darren McGavin, becomes an iconic figure whose eccentricities and obsessions mirror the idiosyncrasies found in many households. His quest to win the "major award" in the form of the leg lamp becomes a humorous commentary on the quirks and priorities that define family life during the holiday season. The interactions between family members, marked by love, exasperation, and genuine moments of connection, mirror the complexity and warmth of real-life family relationships.

Audiences connect with the familial dynamics depicted in "A Christmas Story" because they mirror the universal experiences of growing up in a family, navigating the challenges of sibling relationships, and seeking parental approval. The film's portrayal of family life serves as a mirror reflecting the comedic and heartfelt moments that shape childhood nostalgia.

Imaginative Escapades and Childhood Wonder:

Ralphie's imaginative escapades, particularly his daydreams about owning the Red Ryder BB Gun, become a poignant reminder of the boundless wonder and creativity of childhood. The film captures the essence of a time when a simple desire could fuel elaborate fantasies, transforming mundane moments into grand adventures.

The use of daydream sequences in "A Christmas Story" resonates with audiences who recall the vividness of their own childhood imagination. Whether it's imagining encounters with Black Bart and his gang or envisioning the adulation that would accompany the possession of the coveted BB Gun, Ralphie's daydreams become a nostalgic reminder of the limitless possibilities that define childhood wonder.

The film's exploration of childhood imagination serves as a bridge to the past, prompting viewers to reflect on their own fanciful journeys into the realms of make-believe. Through Ralphie's eyes, audiences are transported to a time when the ordinary became extraordinary, and every day held the potential for magical discoveries.

Challenges of Childhood:

"A Christmas Story" does not shy away from depicting the challenges and trials of childhood. The character of Scut Farkus, the neighborhood bully, becomes a symbolic representation of the obstacles and fears that children often encounter. Ralphie's encounters with Scut Farkus, including the memorable showdown on the schoolyard, resonate with audiences who recall their own experiences of standing up to bullies and facing childhood fears.

The film acknowledges that childhood is not solely defined by joyous moments but also by the struggles and triumphs that shape character. The challenges faced by Ralphie, whether it's navigating schoolyard conflicts or navigating the complexities of adult communication, contribute to the film's authenticity and its ability to connect with the diverse aspects of childhood nostalgia.

Culmination of Relatable Moments:

The brilliance of "A Christmas Story" lies in its ability to string together a series of relatable moments, creating a narrative that encapsulates the multifaceted nature of childhood. Whether it's the arrival of the much-anticipated Little Orphan Annie decoder ring or the humorous challenges of dressing for winter, each scene becomes a snapshot of a shared experience.

The film's episodic structure, framed by the narration of adult Ralphie reflecting on his childhood, allows for the culmination of these relatable moments into a cohesive narrative. The use of adult perspective adds a layer of reflection, prompting audiences to not only relive the specific moments but also to appreciate the broader themes of innocence, resilience, and the enduring spirit of the holiday season.

As audiences revisit "A Christmas Story," they are not merely watching a film; they are revisiting the familiar landscapes of their own childhoods. The culmination of relatable moments creates a tapestry of nostalgia that transcends generational boundaries, allowing the film to resonate with viewers of all ages.

Cinematic Language of Nostalgia:

The cinematic language employed in "A Christmas Story" contributes significantly to its ability to connect with childhood nostalgia. The warm color palette, reminiscent of vintage photographs, evokes a sense of familiarity. The use of voiceover narration by Jean Shepherd, who also appears as an on-screen character, provides a comforting and nostalgic anchor to the narrative.

The film's attention to period-specific details, including costumes, set designs, and props, enhances its nostalgic appeal. The deliberate choice to film in Cleveland, Ohio, where the architecture and landscapes retain a timeless quality, adds to the film's immersive quality. The intentional blend of authenticity and cinematic artifice creates a visual experience that feels both lived-in and dreamlike.

The score, composed by Carl Zittrer, contributes to the film's nostalgic atmosphere. The use of holiday-themed music, including familiar carols and festive tunes, enhances the emotional resonance of key moments. The score becomes a sonic backdrop that elevates the film beyond a mere narrative, creating an auditory landscape that further connects with the emotional chords of childhood nostalgia.

Cultural Endurance and Generational Passing:

The enduring popularity of "A Christmas Story" is a testament to its ability to withstand the test of time and remain relevant across generations. The film's annual television marathons, merchandise featuring iconic quotes and images, and its inclusion in holiday programming schedules reflect its cultural endurance. The passing down of the film from one generation to the next becomes a tradition in itself, solidifying its status as a cherished part of family holiday celebrations.

As parents introduce their children to the adventures of Ralphie Parker, a generational bridge is formed. The film becomes a shared experience, creating a sense of continuity and connection between family members separated by time. The passing down of "A Christmas Story" becomes a rite of passage, with each new generation discovering the film's magic and relatability, further embedding it into the tapestry of childhood nostalgia.

Conclusion:

"A Christmas Story" transcends the boundaries of a holiday film, evolving into a timeless exploration of childhood nostalgia. Its ability to connect with audiences on a deeply personal level is rooted in the universal themes of coming-of-age, relatable family dynamics, imaginative escapades, and the challenges and triumphs of childhood. The film becomes a cinematic conduit to the past, inviting viewers to revisit the cherished moments, traditions, and emotions that define the holiday season and shape the enduring magic of childhood. As audiences continue to return to Hohman, Indiana, with each viewing, "A Christmas Story" remains a beacon of nostalgia, a testament to the enduring power of cinematic storytelling, and a cherished companion on the journey through the timeless landscape of childhood memories.

"A Christmas Story" has carved its place not just in the realm of holiday cinema but within the broader landscape of pop culture, leaving an indelible mark that extends far beyond its initial release. Bob Clark's iconic film, inspired by Jean Shepherd's stories, has become a cultural touchstone, influencing everything from television programming to merchandise and shaping the way audiences engage with and celebrate the holiday season. This exploration delves into the pop culture legacy of "A Christmas Story," examining its enduring impact on entertainment, consumer culture, and the very fabric of holiday traditions.

Annual Tradition and Television Marathons:

One of the most prominent aspects of the pop culture legacy of "A Christmas Story" is its transformation into an annual holiday tradition. The film's journey from theatrical release to becoming a staple of television programming during the holiday season is a testament to its enduring popularity. In 1983, when the film was first released, it performed modestly at the box office. However, its transition to the small screen marked the beginning of a cultural phenomenon.

Television marathons of "A Christmas Story" have become a cherished tradition in many households. Networks, particularly Turner Broadcasting System (TBS), have embraced the film's appeal and dedicated entire days to continuous airings during the Christmas season. The 24-hour marathons, often starting on Christmas Eve and extending into Christmas

Day, have become a ritual for families, providing a backdrop to holiday gatherings and celebrations.

The marathon format not only caters to those who have made it a tradition to watch the film annually but also introduces new generations to the timeless tale of Ralphie's Christmas quest. The decision to air the film continuously for 24 hours has turned "A Christmas Story" into a communal experience, inviting viewers to join in at any point and be part of a collective celebration of holiday nostalgia.

Cult Following and Quotable Moments:

The pop culture legacy of "A Christmas Story" extends beyond its annual television marathons to cultivate a dedicated cult following. The film's status as a cult classic is characterized by the fervent enthusiasm of its fanbase, affectionately known as "Ralphie's Army." The internet age has further fueled this sense of community, with online forums, social media groups, and fan-generated content contributing to the film's enduring relevance.

Central to the film's cult following are its quotable moments, memorable lines, and iconic scenes that have permeated popular culture. Phrases like "You'll shoot your eye out!" and "Oh, fudge!" have become part of the cultural lexicon, transcending the boundaries of the film itself. These quotes are not just recited; they are shared, memed, and woven into everyday conversations, making "A Christmas Story" a linguistic and cultural reference point.

The leg lamp, a symbol of both humor and nostalgia within the film, has achieved iconic status in its own right.

From replicas of the leg lamp becoming popular holiday decorations to references in other forms of media, the leg lamp has become a visual shorthand for the film's unique blend of irreverence and charm.

Merchandising and Consumer Culture:

The pop culture legacy of "A Christmas Story" extends into consumer culture through a wide array of merchandise inspired by the film. From leg lamp nightlights to Red Ryder BB Gun ornaments, the film has inspired a plethora of products that allow fans to incorporate elements of the movie into their holiday celebrations. The intentional kitschiness of some of these items aligns with the film's own sense of humor and contributes to the overall festive spirit.

The success of the film's merchandise is a testament to its ability to resonate with audiences on a personal level. Fans don't just want to watch the film; they want to incorporate its whimsical elements into their own holiday traditions. The leg lamp, in particular, has become a sought-after holiday decoration, with fans proudly displaying their own versions as a nod to the film's enduring charm.

Beyond physical products, the film's impact on consumer culture is evident in its integration into digital platforms. From themed holiday filters on social media to online retailers featuring exclusive "A Christmas Story" collections, the film continues to be a marketable and market-shaping force in the realm of holiday consumerism.

Parodies, Homages, and References:

The cultural influence of "A Christmas Story" is further reflected in the numerous parodies, homages, and references it has inspired across various forms of media. Television shows, films, and even commercials have paid tribute to the iconic moments and characters from the film, embedding its imagery and themes into the broader cultural landscape.

In the realm of television, sitcoms and animated series have often dedicated holiday episodes to riffing on the tropes established by "A Christmas Story." Whether it's the recounting of childhood misadventures, the quest for a coveted item, or the humorous dynamics of family life during the holidays, these episodes draw inspiration from the film's narrative blueprint.

In film, directors and writers have incorporated nods to "A Christmas Story" as a way of acknowledging its cultural significance. Whether through subtle references or direct allusions, the film's influence is evident in works that seek to capture the essence of holiday nostalgia or explore the dynamics of growing up during the festive season.

Commercials, too, have capitalized on the film's recognizable imagery and themes to create memorable holiday advertising campaigns. The leg lamp, in particular, has been featured in commercials for various products, using its distinctive silhouette to evoke immediate associations with the film and the holiday season.

Stage Adaptations and Musical Productions:

The enduring appeal of "A Christmas Story" has led to its adaptation into stage plays and musical productions, further solidifying its presence in the realm of live entertainment. The stage adaptations, often performed during the holiday season, bring the film's characters and narrative to life in a new and interactive way, allowing audiences to experience the story in a different format.

The musical adaptation, titled "A Christmas Story: The Musical," features a score by Benj Pasek and Justin Paul, adding a musical dimension to the film's narrative. The stage productions retain the charm, humor, and heart of the original story while incorporating the dynamics of live performance. The decision to adapt the film for the stage speaks to its enduring popularity and the desire to provide audiences with immersive, multi-sensory experiences during the holiday season.

These stage adaptations not only offer a fresh perspective on the beloved tale but also introduce the story to audiences who may not have encountered the film in its original cinematic form. The decision to bring "A Christmas Story" to the stage underscores its status as a cultural touchstone that can be reimagined and reinterpreted for new generations.

Educational Impact and Classroom Use:

Beyond entertainment and consumer culture, "A Christmas Story" has found a place in educational settings, with teachers incorporating the film into their lesson plans during the holiday season. The film's depiction of a bygone era, its exploration of childhood experiences, and its humorous yet poignant storytelling make it a valuable resource for educators seeking to engage students in discussions about cultural history and narrative techniques.

Teachers often use the film as a springboard for lessons on film analysis, storytelling, and historical context. The period-specific details portrayed in "A Christmas Story" provide a visual and narrative backdrop for discussions about life in America during the 1940s. The film's episodic structure and use of voiceover narration also offer opportunities for students to explore cinematic techniques and storytelling devices.

Moreover, the film's relatable themes, such as the challenges of growing up, familial dynamics, and the quest for identity, resonate with students of various ages. Classroom discussions about the cultural impact of the film, its place in holiday traditions, and its enduring popularity contribute to a broader understanding of how media shapes and reflects cultural values.

Influence on Filmmaking and Holiday Storytelling:

The pop culture legacy of "A Christmas Story" extends to its influence on filmmaking, particularly within the genre of holiday storytelling. The film's success demonstrated the viability of creating holiday-centric narratives that balance humor, nostalgia, and heart. Filmmakers have since looked to "A Christmas Story" as a model for crafting holiday films that resonate with audiences across generations.

The film's episodic structure, where individual scenes contribute to an overarching narrative, has been replicated in various holiday films seeking to capture the essence of the season. The blending of humor with genuine emotional moments, a hallmark of "A Christmas Story," has become a sought-after formula for filmmakers aiming to create enduring and beloved holiday classics.

The film's impact on the genre is evident in the continued production of holiday-themed movies that draw inspiration from its narrative style, thematic elements, and ability to evoke a sense of universal nostalgia. The success of subsequent holiday films owes a debt to the trailblazing spirit of "A Christmas Story," which demonstrated that a holiday movie could be both commercially successful and culturally influential.

Conclusion:

The pop culture legacy of "A Christmas Story" is a testament to its enduring impact on the way audiences engage with the holiday season. From annual television marathons and a dedicated cult following to merchandise, parodies, and educational use, the film has become an integral part of the cultural fabric surrounding Christmas. Its influence extends beyond the realm of cinema, shaping the way we celebrate, reminisce, and pass down traditions to new generations. As "A Christmas Story" continues to be embraced by audiences each holiday season, its pop culture legacy remains a shining example of the lasting power of storytelling to connect, entertain, and become an integral part of our collective holiday memories.

Critical Reconsideration

"A Christmas Story" occupies a unique space in the realm of holiday cinema. Initially met with a modest reception upon its release in 1983, the film has since evolved into a beloved classic, celebrated for its nostalgic charm, humor, and timeless portrayal of childhood during the festive season. This critical reconsideration explores the journey of "A Christmas Story" from its early reviews to its current status as a cultural touchstone, examining the factors that have contributed to its critical reevaluation and enduring appeal.

Initial Critical Reception:

Upon its release, "A Christmas Story" was not an instant blockbuster. Directed by Bob Clark and based on the semi-autobiographical stories of Jean Shepherd, the film faced competition from other holiday releases of the time. Initial critical reviews were mixed, with some praising its nostalgic depiction of 1940s Americana and others finding fault in what they perceived as episodic and disjointed storytelling.

One of the film's early challenges was its unconventional structure. Rather than following a traditional linear narrative, "A Christmas Story" is presented as a series of vignettes, each capturing a specific moment in young Ralphie Parker's quest for a Red Ryder BB Gun. Some critics found this approach disjointed, while others appreciated the episodic nature as a reflection of the original stories by Jean Shepherd.

Critics also highlighted the film's humor, often noting its irreverent take on holiday traditions and family dynamics. The comedic elements, coupled with moments of genuine warmth and heart, created a distinctive tonal balance that divided opinions. The film's refusal to adhere to conventional sentimentality challenged expectations of what a Christmas movie should be, contributing to a range of critical responses.

While the performances, particularly that of a young Peter Billingsley as Ralphie, received praise, some critics found fault with what they perceived as overly exaggerated characters, especially among the adult cast. The portrayal of the Old Man, played by Darren McGavin, and the eccentricities of the Parker family were points of contention, with some reviewers questioning the authenticity of the characters.

Despite these varied responses, "A Christmas Story" did find its champions among critics who appreciated its unconventional approach, witty narration by Jean Shepherd, and ability to capture the essence of childhood nostalgia. However, it was only in the years following its release that the film would undergo a critical reevaluation that would cement its place as a holiday classic.

Cultural Shifts and Audience Connection:

The critical reconsideration of "A Christmas Story" can be attributed, in part, to cultural shifts and changes in audience perception over time. As the years passed, the film found a second life on television, becoming a staple of holiday programming. The decision by networks, particularly TBS, to air 24-hour marathons of the film on Christmas Eve and Christmas Day contributed significantly to its resurgence in popularity.

Television marathons exposed the film to a broader audience, including those who may not have seen it during its theatrical release. The episodic structure, initially a point of contention for some critics, became an asset in the context of television programming. Viewers tuning in at different times throughout the marathon could easily follow and enjoy individual scenes, fostering a communal viewing experience.

The annual tradition of watching "A Christmas Story" became ingrained in the holiday rituals of many families. As new generations discovered and embraced the film, its status as a cultural touchstone solidified. The film's themes of childhood, family, and the quest for a special Christmas gift resonated with audiences of all ages, fostering a sense of shared experience across generations.

The rise of the internet and social media further contributed to the film's critical reconsideration. Online forums, fan communities, and social media platforms became spaces where individuals could express their love for the film, share memes, and participate in discussions about its enduring appeal. The democratization of opinion allowed for a more nuanced and diverse conversation about "A Christmas Story."

Audience members, now equipped with the ability to voice their opinions on a global scale, championed the film's unique qualities. Memorable quotes, iconic scenes, and the relatable portrayal of childhood experiences became focal points of discussion, challenging earlier critical assessments that may have overlooked the film's cultural impact.

Nostalgia and Emotional Resonance:

Nostalgia plays a pivotal role in the critical reconsideration of "A Christmas Story." The film's depiction of 1940s Americana, coupled with its focus on the magic and challenges of childhood, taps into a collective sense of nostalgia for a bygone era. Viewers, especially those who grew up during a time when the film is set, find themselves transported to a world that reflects their own memories and experiences.

The period-specific details, from the Parker family's radio programs to the depiction of department store Santas, contribute to the film's authenticity and resonate with audiences who long for a simpler time. The evocation of nostalgic elements, combined with the timeless themes of family, holiday traditions, and the pursuit of a cherished dream, creates an emotional resonance that transcends generational boundaries.

The emotional impact of "A Christmas Story" lies not only in its humorous escapades but also in its ability to capture the bittersweet essence of growing up. The film acknowledges the challenges and imperfections of family life while celebrating the moments of joy, wonder, and resilience that define childhood. This emotional authenticity, grounded in the experiences of its characters, forms a deep connection with viewers that goes beyond the surface-level humor.

The character of Ralphie, portrayed with earnestness by Peter Billingsley, becomes a relatable protagonist whose aspirations and challenges mirror the universal journey of growing up. Viewers see reflections of their own childhood selves in Ralphie's wide-eyed wonder, his determination to navigate the complexities of family life, and his unwavering belief in the magic of Christmas.

Cinematic Craftsmanship and Directorial Vision:

As the film underwent critical reconsideration, attention also turned to its cinematic craftsmanship and the directorial vision of Bob Clark. While some early reviews may have dismissed the film's episodic structure, subsequent assessments recognized the intentional choices made by Clark to capture the spirit of Jean Shepherd's stories.

The use of voiceover narration, delivered by Jean Shepherd himself, emerged as a crucial storytelling device that added both humor and nostalgic warmth to the film. Shepherd's witty and reflective narration not only guided the audience through Ralphie's escapades but also provided a narrative throughline that tied together the episodic structure. The decision to have Shepherd appear as a character in the film further enhanced its unique narrative style.

The cinematography of "A Christmas Story," under the direction of Clark and cinematographer Reginald H. Morris, contributed to its visual appeal. The film's warm color palette, reminiscent of period photographs, created a visual ambiance that heightened the sense of nostalgia. The deliberate choice to film in Cleveland, Ohio, where timeless architecture and landscapes could evoke the 1940s setting, added to the film's immersive quality.

Clark's direction brought a balance to the film's tonal shifts, allowing for moments of humor, sentimentality, and even a touch of irreverence. The film's ability to seamlessly transition between these tones without losing its emotional core became a hallmark of its directorial vision. The nuanced performances, including those of the child actors who portrayed Ralphie's friends and adversaries, added authenticity to the film's portrayal of childhood.

The decision to embrace humor, even in the face of challenges and imperfections, became a defining characteristic of "A Christmas Story." The film's refusal to adhere to a conventional holiday movie formula allowed it to stand out, offering audiences a refreshing and genuine depiction of the holiday season.

Cultural Impact and Enduring Appeal:

The critical reconsideration of "A Christmas Story" is intrinsically tied to its cultural impact and enduring appeal. The film's journey from a modestly received holiday release to a beloved classic is a testament to its ability to connect with audiences on a deep and personal level. As the film became a cultural phenomenon, its unique qualities and narrative choices were reevaluated through the lens of its lasting influence.

The film's impact extends beyond the realm of cinema, shaping the way audiences engage with the holiday season. The leg lamp, a symbol of the film's irreverent humor, has become an iconic image associated with Christmas decorations. The film's memorable quotes, from "You'll shoot your eye out!" to "Oh, fudge!" are not just lines from a movie; they are cultural touchstones embedded in the collective consciousness.

The decision by TBS to air 24-hour marathons of "A Christmas Story" during the holiday season has become a tradition in itself. Families across the country tune in to watch and rewatch the film, creating a shared experience that transcends individual viewings. The film's presence in holiday programming schedules has elevated it to a position of prominence, ensuring its continued relevance and introduction to new generations.

As online communities and social media platforms have provided spaces for fans to express their love for the film, the critical discourse around "A Christmas Story" has evolved. What may have been initially dismissed as quirks or unconventional choices in the film's narrative and humor are now celebrated as integral to its charm. The film's status as a cultural touchstone has prompted a reevaluation of its place within the broader landscape of holiday cinema.

Conclusion:

The critical reconsideration of "A Christmas Story" reflects not only changes in cultural perception but also the film's ability to stand the test of time. What was once met with mixed reviews has transformed into a holiday classic celebrated for its nostalgic charm, humor, and genuine portrayal of childhood during the Christmas season.

As audiences continue to revisit the film year after year, its enduring appeal becomes increasingly evident. The critical reevaluation acknowledges the intentional choices made by director Bob Clark, the timeless quality of Jean Shepherd's stories, and the film's unique ability to capture the essence of holiday magic and the challenges of growing up.

"A Christmas Story" has become more than a movie; it is a cultural phenomenon that shapes the way we celebrate and reflect on the holiday season. Its critical reconsideration serves as a testament to the enduring power of storytelling to connect with audiences across generations, inviting us to embrace the whimsy, humor, and nostalgia that define the spirit of Christmas in Hohman, Indiana.

"Love Actually" stands as a testament to the power of ensemble storytelling, weaving together a tapestry of interconnected love stories set against the backdrop of the holiday season. Directed by Richard Curtis, this romantic comedy has become a perennial favorite, celebrated for its heartwarming narratives, memorable characters, and, most notably, its exceptional ensemble cast. In this exploration, we delve into the nuances of "Love Actually," examining how its ensemble cast not only contributes to the film's charm but elevates it to the status of a modern holiday classic.

The All-Star Lineup:

"Love Actually" boasts a cast of seasoned actors, rising stars, and established talents, each bringing their unique charisma to the screen. The ensemble cast is a kaleidoscope of characters navigating the complexities of love, showcasing the interconnectedness of their lives during the Christmas season. From romantic leads to quirky supporting roles, the film's cast members contribute to the rich tapestry of stories that unfold, creating a narrative mosaic that resonates with audiences.

The cast includes Hugh Grant as the charismatic Prime Minister, Emma Thompson as the emotionally grounded Karen, Liam Neeson as the grieving widower Daniel, Keira Knightley as the newlywed Juliet, Colin Firth as the lovelorn writer Jamie, and Alan Rickman as the conflicted husband Harry, among others. Each actor brings their A-game, infusing their characters with depth, humor, and authenticity.

Interwoven Narratives:

The brilliance of "Love Actually" lies in its ability to interweave multiple narratives seamlessly. The film employs a mosaic structure, with each character's story forming a piece of a larger, interconnected puzzle. The ensemble cast becomes the glue that binds these diverse narratives together, creating a cohesive and emotionally resonant tapestry.

The characters' lives intersect in unexpected and heartwarming ways, reinforcing the film's central theme that love, in its myriad forms, is the driving force that connects us all. Whether it's the budding romance between the characters played by Martin Freeman and Joanna Page or the poignant friendship between Neeson's Daniel and Thomas Brodie-Sangster's Sam, the ensemble cast ensures that each storyline contributes to the overarching theme of love's transformative power.

The decision to tell multiple love stories simultaneously requires a delicate balance from both the director and the cast. Each character must be distinct yet relatable, and the interactions between them must feel organic. The ensemble cast of "Love Actually" rises to this challenge, creating a cinematic experience where the sum is truly greater than its individual parts.

Hugh Grant's Charming Prime Minister:

As the charismatic Prime Minister David, Hugh Grant delivers a standout performance that adds a touch of humor and charisma to "Love Actually." Grant's portrayal of a leader navigating the complexities of political office and an unexpected attraction to a staff member (played by Martine McCutcheon) provides a lighthearted and entertaining thread to the film.

Grant's natural charm and comedic timing infuse the character of David with a relatable and endearing quality. His dance sequence, set to the tune of "Jump (For My Love)" by The Pointer Sisters, has become an iconic moment in the film, showcasing Grant's ability to balance humor with genuine warmth. The Prime Minister's journey to find love amid political challenges becomes a focal point in the ensemble narrative, contributing to the film's overall sense of joy and optimism.

Emma Thompson's Heartfelt Karen:

Emma Thompson's portrayal of Karen, the devoted wife grappling with her husband's infidelity, adds emotional depth to "Love Actually." Karen's storyline explores the complexities of love, loss, and resilience during the holiday season. Thompson's performance is a masterclass in subtlety and emotional nuance, capturing the quiet strength of a woman facing personal challenges.

The chemistry between Thompson and Alan Rickman, who plays her husband Harry, adds a layer of authenticity to the film. Karen's emotional journey, culminating in the heartbreaking scene where she discovers Harry's betrayal, showcases Thompson's ability to convey complex emotions with grace and vulnerability. The ensemble cast benefits immensely from the emotional weight that Thompson brings to her role, grounding the film in a poignant exploration of love's highs and lows.

Liam Neeson and Thomas Brodie-Sangster's Heartfelt Bond:

The dynamic between Liam Neeson and Thomas Brodie-Sangster forms one of the most touching and heartfelt storylines in "Love Actually." Neeson's portrayal of Daniel, a grieving widower, and Brodie-Sangster's portrayal of his stepson Sam create a narrative thread that explores love in its familial and platonic forms.

Neeson infuses Daniel with a mix of vulnerability, humor, and paternal warmth. His efforts to guide Sam through the challenges of young love, coupled with his own journey of healing, resonates with audiences on a deeply emotional level. Brodie-Sangster's portrayal of Sam, a young boy grappling with the loss of his mother and the pangs of a first crush, adds an element of innocence and sincerity to the film.

The duo's poignant scenes, including the heartfelt airport dash, underscore the film's exploration of love's ability to heal and connect people in unexpected ways. Neeson and Brodie-Sangster contribute to the ensemble cast's ability to evoke a range of emotions, from laughter to tears, within the span of a single storyline.

Colin Firth's Romantic Odyssey:

Colin Firth's character, Jamie, embarks on a romantic odyssey that adds a touch of whimsy and charm to "Love Actually." Firth plays a writer who finds unexpected love in the most unconventional circumstances, and his journey becomes a testament to the serendipitous nature of romance during the holiday season.

Firth's portrayal of Jamie captures both the vulnerability and resilience of someone navigating the complexities of love. The language barrier between Jamie and his love interest, Aurelia (played by Lúcia Moniz), adds a layer of humor to their courtship. Firth's comedic timing, coupled with the genuine chemistry between the characters, contributes to the film's overall celebration of love's ability to transcend barriers.

The iconic scene of Jamie's grand gesture, where he declares his love for Aurelia in Portuguese, has become a standout moment in the film. Firth's performance adds a romantic and endearing quality to the ensemble cast, showcasing the actor's ability to infuse his character with both wit and heart.

Keira Knightley's Nuanced Juliet:

Keira Knightley's portrayal of Juliet, a newlywed caught in a web of unspoken feelings, adds a layer of complexity to "Love Actually." Knightley's performance navigates the delicate balance between the joy of new love and the unspoken tensions that arise in close relationships.

The dynamic between Juliet, her husband Peter (played by Chiwetel Ejiofor), and his best friend Mark (played by Andrew Lincoln) forms a captivating narrative thread. Knightley brings a sense of vulnerability to Juliet, allowing audiences to empathize with her internal struggle. The use of music, particularly the iconic doorstep scene set to the melody of "Silent Night," underscores the emotional nuances of Knightley's performance.

Knightley's presence in the ensemble cast adds a layer of modernity to the film, exploring themes of unrequited love and the complexities of relationships in a changing world. Her nuanced portrayal contributes to the film's ability to resonate with audiences who may find aspects of their own romantic experiences reflected in Juliet's journey.

Alan Rickman's Complex Harry:

Alan Rickman's portrayal of Harry, the conflicted husband facing temptation, adds a layer of moral ambiguity to "Love Actually." Rickman's performance explores the complexities of love within the context of long-term relationships, infidelity, and the consequences of one's choices.

The chemistry between Rickman and Emma Thompson, who plays his wife Karen, creates a believable portrayal of a couple facing the challenges of maintaining connection in the midst of life's pressures. Rickman's ability to convey both charm and internal conflict adds depth to the character of Harry, challenging audiences to consider the complexities of love and loyalty.

The narrative arc involving Harry's temptation and its impact on his marriage adds a layer of realism to the film, acknowledging that love is not always straightforward or without challenges. Rickman's performance, marked by subtle gestures and expressions, contributes to the ensemble cast's exploration of love in its various shades.

The Chemistry That Elevates the Film:

One of the standout achievements of "Love Actually" is the palpable chemistry among its ensemble cast. Whether through comedic banter, tender moments, or heart-wrenching revelations, the interactions between characters feel authentic and resonant. The chemistry among the cast members elevates the film beyond a collection of individual stories, creating a cohesive and emotionally impactful narrative.

The camaraderie among the actors extends beyond the screen, evident in interviews and behind-the-scenes footage. The genuine affection and rapport among the ensemble cast contribute to the film's overall sense of joy and camaraderie. This chemistry is particularly evident in scenes where characters' lives intersect, emphasizing the interconnected nature of their stories.

The decision to assemble such a talented and diverse cast pays dividends in the film's ability to capture the complexities of love in its various forms. The ensemble cast brings depth, authenticity, and emotional resonance to their respective roles, ensuring that each character contributes meaningfully to the overarching theme of love during the holiday season.

Impact on the Romantic Comedy Genre:

"Love Actually" has had a lasting impact on the romantic comedy genre, influencing subsequent films that explore interconnected love stories. The success of the ensemble cast formula showcased in "Love Actually" has become a template for filmmakers seeking to capture the magic of love through multiple narrative threads.

The film's ability to balance humor, heart, and a touch of melancholy has set a standard for romantic comedies that aspire to be both entertaining and emotionally resonant. Filmmakers have looked to "Love Actually" as a model for crafting stories that celebrate the complexities of love, acknowledging that relationships are multifaceted and often defy traditional conventions.

The ensemble cast approach, popularized by "Love Actually," has become a subgenre within romantic comedies, with subsequent films seeking to replicate the film's success. While many have attempted to capture the magic of interconnected love stories, "Love Actually" remains a touchstone in the genre, admired for its authenticity, wit, and ability to evoke a range of emotions.

Conclusion:

"Love Actually" stands as a shining example of how an ensemble cast can elevate a film from a collection of individual narratives to a cohesive and emotionally resonant experience. The chemistry, talent, and dedication of the cast members contribute to the film's enduring popularity, making it a staple of holiday movie-watching.

The ensemble cast's ability to navigate the complexities of love, from the whimsical to the profound, creates a cinematic mosaic that reflects the diversity of human connections. Each actor brings a unique flavor to the film, contributing to the overall charm and impact of "Love Actually." As audiences continue to revisit the film year after year, its ensemble cast remains a driving force in its timeless appeal, proving that when it comes to love, the more, the merrier.

Heartwarming Romantic Stories

"Love Actually" transcends the typical romantic comedy, offering a cinematic bouquet of heartwarming love stories that unfold against the enchanting backdrop of Christmas. Directed by Richard Curtis, the film artfully weaves together narratives that explore the many facets of love, from the whimsical to the poignant. In this exploration, we delve into the heartwarming romantic stories that have made "Love Actually" a perennial favorite, capturing the essence of love in its myriad forms.

Mark and Juliet's Unspoken Affection:

One of the most iconic and subtly poignant storylines in "Love Actually" revolves around Mark (played by Andrew Lincoln), Juliet (Keira Knightley), and Peter (Chiwetel Ejiofor). Mark's unspoken affection for Juliet, his best friend Peter's wife, forms a narrative thread that unfolds through small yet impactful gestures.

Mark's profession of love takes an unconventional form: a series of cue cards expressing his feelings. This silent declaration, set to the tune of Dido's "Here with Me," becomes a cinematic moment that resonates with audiences. The use of cue cards allows Mark to communicate his emotions without disrupting the established relationships, adding a layer of bittersweetness to the narrative.

This heartwarming storyline explores the complexities of unrequited love, sacrifice, and the acceptance of one's emotions. Andrew Lincoln's portrayal of Mark captures the nuances of silent yearning, while Keira Knightley's Juliet navigates the realization of Mark's feelings with sensitivity and grace. The resolution of this storyline, marked by a gesture of mutual understanding, contributes to the film's overall celebration of love's transformative power.

Jamie and Aurelia's Language of Love:

Colin Firth's character, Jamie, embarks on a romantic odyssey that is both charming and heartwarming. His love story with Aurelia (Lúcia Moniz) unfolds in a series of humorous and endearing moments, overcoming language barriers and cultural differences.

The initial awkwardness between Jamie, an Englishman, and Aurelia, a Portuguese housekeeper, adds a layer of humor to their courtship. The film embraces the notion that love can transcend linguistic challenges, a theme reinforced by the characters' determination to understand each other despite not sharing a common language.

The iconic scene where Jamie proposes to Aurelia in broken Portuguese captures the essence of their love story. The use of humor, coupled with genuine emotion, elevates their romance beyond conventional tropes. Colin Firth and Lúcia Moniz infuse their characters with warmth and authenticity, making Jamie and Aurelia's love story a standout in the ensemble of "Love Actually."

Daniel and Sam's Journey Through Grief:

The relationship between Liam Neeson's character, Daniel, and his stepson Sam (Thomas Brodie-Sangster) forms a poignant and heartwarming narrative within "Love Actually." The storyline explores themes of grief, the resilience of familial bonds, and the transformative power of love.

Daniel, still mourning the loss of his wife, navigates the challenges of parenting Sam, a young boy grappling with the absence of his mother. The film delicately balances moments of humor with genuine emotional weight, capturing the duo's journey through grief and healing.

Thomas Brodie-Sangster's portrayal of Sam adds a layer of innocence and sincerity to the film. His pursuit of love, inspired by his stepfather's guidance, becomes a testament to the enduring nature of love even in the face of loss. Neeson's performance brings depth to Daniel, portraying a father figure who not only provides guidance but also learns valuable lessons from his son.

The heartfelt airport dash, where Sam races to express his feelings to his crush, becomes a climactic moment that reinforces the film's central theme of love's ability to overcome obstacles. The father-son dynamic between Neeson and Brodie-Sangster contributes to the film's emotional resonance and underscores the various forms that love can take.

Karen and Harry's Complex Journey:

Emma Thompson and Alan Rickman portray Karen and Harry, a couple facing the challenges of a long-term relationship. Their storyline delves into the complexities of love, betrayal, and the impact of choices on a marriage.

The film navigates the delicate territory of infidelity as Harry becomes entangled in a workplace temptation. Emma Thompson's performance as Karen is a masterclass in emotional subtlety, conveying the heartbreak of a spouse discovering betrayal while maintaining a facade for the sake of their children.

Alan Rickman brings depth to the character of Harry, portraying a man torn between desire and commitment. The film's exploration of infidelity is marked by nuance, presenting the characters as imperfect individuals facing the complexities of long-term relationships. The impact of Harry's choices reverberates through the narrative, adding a layer of realism to the film's portrayal of love's challenges.

The scene where Karen discovers Harry's secret becomes a powerful moment of emotional revelation. Thompson's portrayal captures the quiet devastation of betrayal, making it a standout moment in the film. The resolution of Karen and Harry's storyline, marked by a poignant family Christmas, offers a glimpse into the complexities of forgiveness and the enduring nature of familial love.

Prime Minister David and Natalie's Whimsical Romance:

Hugh Grant's portrayal of Prime Minister David adds a touch of whimsy to "Love Actually," as his character navigates the challenges of political office and an unexpected attraction to Natalie (Martine McCutcheon). Their storyline combines humor with genuine romantic moments, contributing to the film's overall sense of joy.

The film embraces the idea of love blossoming in unexpected places, in this case, within the confines of political power dynamics. Hugh Grant's charismatic performance infuses David with a relatable charm, while Martine

McCutcheon's portrayal of Natalie adds a blend of innocence and sass to their dynamic.

The dance sequence, where Prime Minister David takes to the dance floor to express his feelings, has become an iconic moment in the film. This whimsical portrayal of political and romantic liberation captures the spirit of the film and reinforces its central theme of love breaking through societal norms.

The resolution of David and Natalie's storyline, marked by a public declaration of affection, contributes to the film's overall celebration of love's ability to triumph over external obstacles. The lighthearted and charming nature of their romance adds a layer of optimism to "Love Actually."

Sarah, Karl, and the Unspoken Love:

Laura Linney's character, Sarah, grapples with the challenges of unrequited love in the workplace, adding a poignant layer to "Love Actually." Her storyline explores the sacrifices and internal conflicts that can accompany unspoken feelings, even in the midst of the holiday season.

Sarah's affection for Karl (Rodrigo Santoro) remains unexpressed as she prioritizes her responsibilities as a caregiver for her mentally ill brother. The film presents a nuanced portrayal of love that goes beyond romantic relationships, acknowledging the sacrifices individuals make for family and personal well-being.

Laura Linney's performance captures the internal struggle of balancing personal desires with familial responsibilities. The film treats Sarah's storyline with sensitivity, acknowledging the complexity of love in its various forms. The resolution of her narrative, marked by a silent phone call, underscores the film's exploration of the multifaceted nature of love.

The Overarching Theme of Love:

"Love Actually" succeeds not just in telling individual romantic stories but in creating a cohesive narrative that explores love in all its forms. The film's strength lies in its ability to depict love as a multifaceted and transformative force that permeates various aspects of life.

From familial love to romantic entanglements, the film navigates the complexities of human relationships with humor, warmth, and a touch of melancholy. Each romantic storyline contributes to the overarching theme of love's ability to bring joy, healing, and understanding, even in the face of challenges.

The interconnectedness of the characters and their stories reinforces the idea that love, in its many expressions, binds individuals together. The film celebrates the diversity of love, portraying it as a force that transcends societal norms, cultural barriers, and personal hardships.

Impact on Audience Emotions:

"Love Actually" has a unique ability to elicit a range of emotions from its audience. The heartwarming romantic stories, marked by moments of humor, tenderness, and emotional resonance, create a cinematic experience that resonates with viewers on a personal level.

The film's impact on audience emotions is heightened by its relatable characters and universal themes. Viewers see reflections of their own experiences, whether in the excitement of new love, the challenges of long-term relationships, or the complexities of familial bonds. The emotional authenticity of the characters allows audiences to empathize with their journeys, fostering a deep connection to the film's overarching celebration of love.

The moments of heartwarming romance, punctuated by memorable scenes and iconic lines, linger in the hearts of viewers long after the credits roll. "Love Actually" becomes not just a film to watch but an emotional experience that invites audiences to reflect on their own relationships and connections.

Cultural Impact and Enduring Appeal:

"Love Actually" has left an indelible mark on popular culture, becoming a staple of holiday movie-watching. The heartwarming romantic stories, coupled with the film's enduring appeal, have contributed to its status as a modern classic.

The film's impact extends beyond the screen, influencing the way audiences approach love and relationships during the holiday season. Iconic moments, such as the cue card scene and the Prime Minister's dance, have become cultural touchstones that are referenced and celebrated in various forms of media.

As an annual tradition for many during the holiday season, "Love Actually" continues to captivate new generations of viewers. Its timeless exploration of love, coupled with heartwarming romantic stories, ensures its enduring place in the pantheon of beloved films.

Conclusion:

"Love Actually" stands as a testament to the power of heartwarming romantic stories in cinema. The film's ability to navigate the complexities of love, from the whimsical to the profound, creates a cinematic experience that resonates with audiences on a deep and emotional level.

The interconnected narratives, each exploring a different facet of love, contribute to the film's overarching celebration of this universal and transformative force. Whether through silent gestures, grand romantic gestures, or the resilience of familial bonds, "Love Actually" captures the essence of love in all its forms.

As audiences continue to revisit the film year after year, the heartwarming romantic stories within "Love Actually" remain a source of joy, laughter, and heartfelt emotion. The film's enduring appeal lies in its ability to evoke the timeless and universal nature of love, making it a cherished and essential part of the holiday movie tradition.

"Love Actually" masterfully employs the art of storytelling through cleverly tied together vignettes, creating a narrative tapestry that explores the diverse facets of love during the Christmas season. Richard Curtis, the director and writer, showcases his adeptness at interweaving multiple storylines, each with its unique charm and resonance. In this exploration, we delve into the brilliance of the film's structure, examining how these cleverly tied together vignettes contribute to the richness and depth of "Love Actually."

The Mosaic of Love:

"Love Actually" is renowned for its mosaic-like structure, presenting a series of interconnected stories that unfold concurrently. This narrative approach allows the film to capture the breadth of love in its various forms, from romantic entanglements to familial bonds. The clever interplay between these vignettes creates a cinematic experience where the sum is undeniably greater than its individual parts.

The film's opening sequence at Heathrow Airport sets the stage for the interconnectedness of the characters. As real-life footage captures the heartwarming reunions of loved ones, the voiceover reflects on the omnipresence of love, establishing the overarching theme that threads through each vignette. This thematic throughline serves as the glue that binds the diverse stories together, ensuring a cohesive and emotionally resonant viewing experience.

The Prime Minister and the Staffer:

One of the central vignettes revolves around Prime Minister David (Hugh Grant) and Natalie (Martine McCutcheon), a member of the household staff at 10 Downing Street. Their storyline cleverly navigates the complexities of workplace romance and the challenges posed by societal expectations.

The film introduces the audience to the subtle flirtations and awkward encounters between David and Natalie, adding a touch of humor to their budding romance. The clever use of misdirection, such as the initial assumption that Natalie is merely a junior staff member, keeps the audience engaged and invested in their evolving dynamic.

The revelation of David's true feelings for Natalie during the Christmas play captures the essence of their relationship. The public declaration of affection, defying the norms of political decorum, becomes a poignant and cleverly executed moment that resonates throughout the film. This vignette not only explores the theme of love in unexpected places but also contributes to the film's overall celebration of breaking societal norms for the sake of genuine connection.

Mark's Silent Affection:

Mark's unspoken love for Juliet (Keira Knightley) represents one of the most cleverly nuanced vignettes in "Love Actually." Using cue cards to express his feelings, Mark's silent affection becomes a powerful exploration of unrequited love, sacrifice, and the acceptance of personal boundaries.

The film cleverly builds tension around Mark's unspoken emotions, leaving the audience to speculate about the nature of his feelings. The use of cue cards serves as an inventive and memorable cinematic device, allowing Mark to communicate his emotions without verbalizing them. This clever twist elevates the emotional impact of the revelation, making it a standout moment in the film.

The resolution of this vignette, where Juliet discovers Mark's silent confession and acknowledges it with a knowing smile, showcases the film's ability to balance melancholy with moments of understanding. Mark's silent affection becomes a clever exploration of the complexities of love, adding depth to the overall narrative.

Jamie and Aurelia's Cross-Cultural Romance:

Colin Firth's character, Jamie, embarks on a cross-cultural romance with Aurelia (Lúcia Moniz), a Portuguese housekeeper. This vignette cleverly navigates language barriers, cultural differences, and the whimsical nature of falling in love in unexpected circumstances.

The film employs humor and charm to portray the initial awkwardness between Jamie and Aurelia, as they navigate their burgeoning attraction despite not sharing a common language. This clever use of comedy adds levity to their romance, making it relatable and endearing to audiences.

The language barrier becomes a poignant metaphor for the challenges of love, and the film cleverly uses this element to highlight the universal nature of romantic connections. Jamie's grand gesture, where he learns Portuguese to express his feelings, serves as a clever resolution that reinforces the film's theme of love transcending boundaries.

Daniel and Sam's Heartfelt Bond:

The relationship between Liam Neeson's character, Daniel, and his stepson Sam (Thomas Brodie-Sangster) forms a heartfelt and cleverly executed vignette. Their narrative explores themes of grief, resilience, and the transformative power of familial love.

The film cleverly balances moments of humor with genuine emotional weight as Daniel guides Sam through the challenges of young love while dealing with his own grief. The use of humor, such as Sam's pursuit of love through the ingenious drumming scheme, adds a clever touch to their storyline, making it relatable and endearing.

The resolution of their narrative, marked by the poignant airport dash, cleverly reinforces the film's central theme of love overcoming obstacles. The heartwarming bond between Daniel and Sam becomes a narrative anchor that cleverly ties together the broader tapestry of "Love Actually."

Karen and Harry's Complex Dynamics:

The vignette involving Karen (Emma Thompson) and Harry (Alan Rickman) cleverly navigates the complexities of long-term relationships, infidelity, and the consequences of choices. The film presents a nuanced exploration of love in the face of betrayal, adding depth to the overall narrative.

Clever misdirection is employed to gradually reveal Harry's infidelity, keeping the audience emotionally invested in the unraveling dynamics of Karen and Harry's marriage. The cleverly written and performed scenes leading to Karen's discovery create a sense of emotional suspense that underscores the film's exploration of love's challenges.

The resolution of Karen and Harry's storyline, marked by a bittersweet family Christmas, cleverly subverts traditional expectations. The film chooses to emphasize the enduring nature of familial love despite the complexities of romantic relationships. This vignette cleverly adds a layer of emotional complexity to the film's overarching theme.

Sarah's Unspoken Sacrifice:

Laura Linney's character, Sarah, contributes a poignant and cleverly tied together vignette that explores unspoken sacrifices for familial love. Her narrative cleverly delves into the challenges of balancing personal desires with responsibilities, showcasing the multifaceted nature of love.

The film cleverly builds tension around Sarah's unexpressed feelings for Karl (Rodrigo Santoro), intertwining her desire for romance with her role as a caregiver for her mentally ill brother. This narrative choice adds a layer of emotional complexity to Sarah's character, making her storyline relatable and emotionally resonant.

The cleverly written resolution, marked by a silent phone call and Sarah's choice to prioritize her brother over personal desires, reinforces the film's exploration of love in its various forms. Sarah's vignette becomes a powerful and cleverly executed component of "Love Actually."

The Ensemble Cast's Interconnectedness:

The brilliance of "Love Actually" lies in its ability to showcase the interconnectedness of its ensemble cast. The film cleverly intertwines the characters' lives, allowing their stories to intersect in subtle and meaningful ways. This interconnectedness reinforces the film's central theme of love as a force that binds individuals together, transcending individual narratives.

The use of recurring motifs, such as the holiday season and music, cleverly ties together the various vignettes, creating a cohesive and emotionally resonant viewing experience. Whether through visual cues or thematic echoes, the film ensures that each character's journey contributes to the overarching narrative of love during the Christmas season.

The Impact of Clever Storytelling:

The cleverly tied together vignettes in "Love Actually" have a profound impact on the audience. The interplay between humor and heartfelt moments, coupled with the film's thematic cohesion, creates a narrative experience that is both engaging and emotionally resonant.

The clever storytelling choices, such as the use of misdirection, visual motifs, and thematic throughlines, elevate "Love Actually" beyond a conventional romantic comedy. The film's structure allows viewers to become emotionally invested in multiple characters and their journeys, fostering a deeper connection to the overarching theme of love.

Clever storytelling also allows the film to explore the complexities of love in its various forms—romantic, familial, and unrequited. By presenting a mosaic of interconnected stories, "Love Actually" captures the richness and diversity of human relationships, ensuring that audiences see reflections of their own experiences on screen.

Legacy of Clever Storytelling:

"Love Actually" has left an enduring legacy in the realm of romantic comedies, showcasing the impact of cleverly tied together vignettes on storytelling. The film's success has influenced subsequent works, inspiring filmmakers to explore interconnected narratives and thematic cohesion in their storytelling.

The legacy of clever storytelling in "Love Actually" is evident in its enduring popularity and cultural resonance. Viewers continue to revisit the film not only for its heartwarming romantic stories but also for the clever and nuanced way in which these stories are interwoven.

As a modern classic, "Love Actually" stands as a testament to the enduring power of cleverly tied together vignettes in capturing the complexities of love, especially during the magical and transformative Christmas season.

Conclusion:

"Love Actually" stands as a shining example of the art of storytelling through cleverly tied together vignettes. The film's mosaic-like structure, thematic cohesion, and interconnected narratives create a cinematic experience that is both heartwarming and intellectually engaging. The brilliance of the film lies in its ability to explore the diverse facets of love, from the whimsical to the profound, through a cleverly crafted tapestry of interconnected stories.

As audiences continue to embrace and celebrate "Love Actually" during the holiday season, its legacy as a masterclass in clever storytelling remains intact. The film's impact on the romantic comedy genre, its enduring popularity, and its cultural resonance all attest to the timeless appeal of stories that cleverly weave together the threads of love in all its beautiful complexity.

Is It Actually a Christmas Movie?

The debate surrounding what qualifies as a "Christmas movie" has been a perennial topic of discussion among film enthusiasts, and "Love Actually" finds itself nestled in the heart of this ongoing conversation. As a film that weaves together romantic narratives against the backdrop of the Christmas season, it prompts us to explore the question: Is "Love Actually" actually a Christmas movie?

The Christmas Setting:

One of the primary arguments in favor of "Love Actually" being a Christmas movie is, undeniably, its setting. The film unfolds during the weeks leading up to Christmas, utilizing the festive season as more than just a backdrop. The holiday spirit permeates every frame, from the bustling streets adorned with Christmas decorations to the ubiquitous sounds of carols and festive tunes that punctuate the soundtrack.

The Christmas setting serves not only as a visual and auditory feast for the audience but also as a narrative device that shapes and influences the characters' actions and decisions. The emphasis on gift-giving, family gatherings, and the magic of the season becomes integral to the storytelling, aligning "Love Actually" with the quintessential elements of Christmas movies.

The Theme of Love and Connection:

At the heart of "Love Actually" lies a thematic resonance that aligns with the spirit of Christmas: the celebration of love and connection. The film explores various forms of love—romantic, familial, and platonic—underscoring the idea that the holiday season is a time for people to come together and express their affection for one another.

Each vignette within the film contributes to this overarching theme of love. Whether it's the romantic entanglements of characters like Jamie and Aurelia or the familial bonds explored through characters like Daniel and Sam, the film weaves a narrative tapestry that celebrates the transformative power of love, a sentiment synonymous with the Christmas season.

The culmination of these love stories, often marked by heartwarming resolutions and reunions, reinforces the film's alignment with the emotional and thematic core of Christmas movies. Viewers are left with a sense of warmth and joy, much like the feelings associated with the holiday season.

Christmas Traditions and Rituals:

"Love Actually" further solidifies its claim as a Christmas movie through its portrayal of traditional festive elements and rituals. The film captures the essence of Christmas traditions, whether it's the decorating of homes, the exchange of gifts, or the joyful anticipation of the holiday itself.

The opening scene at Heathrow Airport, featuring real footage of reunions during the Christmas season, becomes a poignant nod to the tradition of coming together with loved ones during this time of year. The film cleverly incorporates these traditions, making them integral to the narrative and reinforcing the connection between "Love Actually" and the Christmas movie genre.

Iconic Christmas Moments:

Certain scenes within "Love Actually" have attained iconic status, further contributing to the argument that the film qualifies as a Christmas classic. The Prime Minister's dance to "Jump (For My Love)" becomes a memorable and lighthearted Christmas moment, injecting a sense of joy and festivity into the narrative.

The nativity play featuring Sam and Joanna adds a charming and distinctly Christmas touch, showcasing the innocence and magic associated with the holiday season. The film strategically places these iconic Christmas moments, creating a visual and emotional resonance that aligns with the expectations of audiences seeking a quintessential Christmas movie experience.

Holiday Soundtrack:

Music plays a pivotal role in defining the atmosphere of "Love Actually," and the film's soundtrack is particularly noteworthy for its inclusion of classic Christmas songs. From the opening notes of "Christmas Is All Around" performed by Billy Mack (Bill Nighy) to the soul-stirring rendition of "All I Want for Christmas Is You" by Olivia Olson's character, Joanna, the soundtrack becomes a melodic celebration of the Christmas spirit.

The incorporation of these festive tunes not only enhances the film's thematic connection to Christmas but also creates a sonic landscape that resonates with the joy and nostalgia associated with the holiday season. The strategic use of holiday music further cements "Love Actually" as a film intricately tied to the Christmas movie tradition.

A Counterargument:

However, amid the festive trimmings and heartwarming narratives, there exists a counterargument questioning the classification of "Love Actually" as a Christmas movie. Detractors argue that the film's exploration of love is not exclusive to the Christmas season and that the holiday serves more as a backdrop than a central narrative element.

Additionally, the film's depiction of love in various forms, including romantic entanglements and familial bonds, is considered by some as a universal theme that transcends the specific context of Christmas. Critics argue that the film could unfold during any time of the year without losing its thematic essence.

The Year-Round Appeal:

Those who challenge the designation of "Love Actually" as a Christmas movie often point to its year-round appeal. Unlike traditional Christmas movies that are typically reserved for holiday viewing, "Love Actually" has found a place in the hearts of audiences throughout the entire calendar.

The film's exploration of love, humor, and human relationships resonates irrespective of the season, making it a perennial favorite for moviegoers. The argument here is that a true Christmas movie should be inseparable from the holiday experience, and "Love Actually" is a film that transcends its Christmas setting to offer a narrative that can be enjoyed year-round.

The Love Actually Controversy:

The debate over whether "Love Actually" is a Christmas movie has become a cultural touchpoint, sparking discussions and social media debates every holiday season. The film's enduring popularity and its inclusion in numerous holiday movie lists contribute to the ongoing discourse.

Part of the controversy stems from the evolving definition of what constitutes a Christmas movie. Traditionally, films like "It's a Wonderful Life" or "A Christmas Carol" are unequivocally categorized as Christmas movies due to their thematic focus on the holiday. "Love Actually," with its blend of romance, humor, and Christmas elements, challenges these traditional categorizations.

In Defense of the Christmas Movie Label:

Despite the counterarguments, supporters of the Christmas movie label for "Love Actually" find strength in its enduring popularity as a holiday season staple. The film has become a cultural phenomenon, with fans eagerly anticipating its annual rewatch as part of their Christmas traditions.

The undeniable association of "Love Actually" with the festive season, both in terms of narrative and thematic elements, makes it a strong contender for the Christmas movie designation. The film's enduring popularity, the abundance of Christmas traditions depicted, and its ability to evoke the holiday spirit collectively contribute to its status as a beloved Christmas classic.

Conclusion:

In the end, whether "Love Actually" is deemed a Christmas movie may hinge on individual perspectives and the criteria one uses to define the genre. The film undoubtedly captures the magic, traditions, and thematic essence of Christmas, making it a heartwarming and joyous viewing experience during the holiday season.

The ongoing debate surrounding "Love Actually" adds to its mystique, ensuring that the film remains a topic of discussion and reflection each Christmas. Whether viewed as a Christmas movie or a film that transcends seasonal categorizations, "Love Actually" has undeniably earned its place in the pantheon of beloved films, creating a unique and enduring legacy in the realm of holiday cinema.

"The Polar Express" stands as a cinematic marvel, not only for its enchanting narrative and festive charm but also for its groundbreaking use of motion capture technology. Directed by Robert Zemeckis, the film, based on Chris Van Allsburg's beloved children's book, pushed the boundaries of what was possible in animation and filmmaking, particularly with its innovative approach to motion capture.

Introduction to Motion Capture:

Before delving into the specifics of "The Polar Express," it's essential to understand the concept of motion capture. Motion capture, often abbreviated as mocap, is a filmmaking technique that records the movements of actors, typically using sensors or markers attached to their bodies. These movements are then translated into digital animations, creating lifelike and realistic characters.

The primary goal of motion capture is to bridge the gap between live-action performances and animated characters, providing a level of realism and nuance that traditional animation techniques might not achieve. It has been widely used in various genres, from action films to animated features, but "The Polar Express" marked a significant leap forward in its application.

The Technological Leap in "The Polar Express":

Released in 2004, "The Polar Express" was one of the first feature-length films to extensively use motion capture technology for creating its characters. Unlike earlier attempts that relied on live-action performances to animate characters or limited motion capture for specific sequences, "The Polar Express" embraced motion capture as its primary animation technique.

The film utilized a state-of-the-art motion capture system developed by Sony Pictures Imageworks, capturing the performances of actors in incredible detail. This system involved placing reflective markers on the actors' bodies, which were then tracked by cameras in a controlled studio environment. The captured data were then used to create digital models of the characters, preserving the nuances of the actors' performances.

Achieving Realism in Animation:

One of the primary challenges in animation has always been achieving realistic human movements and expressions. Traditional animation, while capable of incredible artistry, often struggled to replicate the subtleties of human motion. Motion capture presented an opportunity to address this challenge by directly translating the movements of real actors into the digital realm.

In "The Polar Express," this translated to characters that exhibited a level of realism previously unseen in animated films. The use of motion capture allowed for the faithful recreation of facial expressions, body language, and even the imperfections that make human movement authentic. This commitment to realism was particularly crucial in a film like "The Polar Express," where conveying genuine emotion and connection was central to the narrative.

The Characters of "The Polar Express":

The success of motion capture in "The Polar Express" is evident in the lifelike and expressive characters that populate the film. From the wide-eyed and curious Hero Boy (voiced by Daryl Sabara) to the enigmatic and whimsical conductor (voiced by Tom Hanks), each character is brought to life with a level of detail and nuance that captivated audiences.

The film's protagonist, voiced and motion-captured by Tom Hanks, is not just a digital representation of an animated character; he is a faithful recreation of the actor's performance. The technology allowed for the seamless integration of Hanks' expressive acting into the character, capturing the warmth and humanity of the performance.

The use of motion capture also extended to other characters, such as the eccentric know-it-all boy, the shy and sweet Hero Girl, and, notably, Santa Claus himself. The technology facilitated the creation of characters with distinct personalities and a level of authenticity that resonated with audiences, contributing to the film's emotional impact.

Creating a Digital Wonderland:

Beyond characters, motion capture played a pivotal role in crafting the visual spectacle of "The Polar Express." The film's magical setting, from the interiors of the enchanting train to the snowy landscapes of the North Pole, was brought to life with meticulous detail and a sense of wonder.

The motion capture technology allowed the filmmakers to choreograph intricate and visually stunning sequences, such as the dynamic train ride or the bustling activity at the North

Pole workshop. The fluidity of motion capture translated into a sense of dynamism and realism in the animation, enhancing the overall cinematic experience.

The film's expressive and lively animation style was a departure from traditional holiday specials, offering audiences a visually immersive journey into a digital wonderland. The characters' movements, whether dancing, laughing, or expressing awe, were not constrained by the limitations of traditional animation, resulting in a film that felt both magical and authentic.

Overcoming Technical Challenges:

While motion capture provided unprecedented opportunities for realism, its implementation in "The Polar Express" was not without challenges. The technology was relatively new on such a large scale, and the filmmakers had to navigate technical complexities to ensure the success of the project.

One notable challenge was the "uncanny valley" phenomenon, wherein characters that are almost, but not quite, realistic can evoke a sense of unease in viewers. Striking the right balance between realism and stylization was crucial to ensure that the characters in "The Polar Express" felt endearing rather than unsettling. The filmmakers addressed this challenge through careful character design and animation choices.

The complexity of capturing performances in a three-dimensional space also posed logistical challenges. The actors had to wear motion capture suits and perform in a controlled environment, which could be restrictive compared to traditional live-action filming. However, the benefits of achieving lifelike character animations outweighed these challenges, allowing the filmmakers to deliver a visually groundbreaking and emotionally resonant film.

Impact on Filmmaking:

"The Polar Express" left an indelible mark on the landscape of animated filmmaking, particularly in its impact on the use of motion capture. The success of the film showcased the potential of this technology in creating immersive and emotionally engaging animated experiences.

Following "The Polar Express," Robert Zemeckis continued to explore the possibilities of motion capture in films like "Beowulf" and "A Christmas Carol." The technology became a signature element of Zemeckis's directorial style, and its influence extended to other filmmakers who recognized its potential for storytelling.

Motion capture technology has since become a staple in the animation industry, evolving and improving with each passing year. Filmmakers have embraced it for various genres, from fantasy epics to character-driven dramas. The lessons learned from "The Polar Express" paved the way for advancements in motion capture, contributing to its widespread adoption in contemporary filmmaking.

Legacy of "The Polar Express":

"The Polar Express" remains a testament to the power of innovation in filmmaking. Beyond its heartwarming story and memorable characters, the film is celebrated for its groundbreaking use of motion capture, which redefined the possibilities of animation.

The legacy of "The Polar Express" extends to its influence on subsequent animated films and the broader conversation about the intersection of technology and storytelling. The film's success demonstrated that animation could transcend traditional boundaries and deliver a cinematic experience that rivaled live-action filmmaking in emotional impact and visual spectacle.

As audiences continue to embark on the magical journey of "The Polar Express" during the holiday season, they do so with an appreciation for the technological marvel that brought the beloved story to life. The film's pioneering use of motion capture remains a milestone in the history of animated cinema, a testament to the spirit of innovation that defines the magic of the movies.

Sense of Childlike Wonder

"The Polar Express" is a cinematic journey that transcends the boundaries between reality and fantasy, inviting audiences of all ages to rediscover the enchantment and sense of childlike wonder that defines the holiday season. Directed by Robert Zemeckis and based on Chris Van Allsburg's beloved book, the film captures the magic of Christmas through its immersive storytelling, breathtaking animation, and the evocation of a timeless sense of childlike wonder.

Immersive Storytelling:

At the heart of "The Polar Express" is a narrative that captures the essence of childhood wonder and imagination. The story follows a young boy, known simply as Hero Boy, on a magical train journey to the North Pole on Christmas Eve. This fantastical adventure unfolds with a sense of mystery and anticipation, reminiscent of the excitement that children feel during the holiday season.

The immersive storytelling of "The Polar Express" taps into universal themes of belief, courage, and the spirit of Christmas. As Hero Boy embarks on this extraordinary journey, the film weaves a tapestry of emotions and experiences that resonate with viewers of all ages. The narrative unfolds with a gentle nostalgia, harkening back to the timeless tales that have enchanted generations of readers and audiences.

Visual Splendor and Animation:

A key contributor to the sense of childlike wonder in "The Polar Express" is its visually stunning animation. The film leverages state-of-the-art technology, including groundbreaking motion capture, to create a world that sparkles with magic and captivates the imagination. From the intricately detailed train to the snowy landscapes of the North Pole, every frame is a testament to the film's commitment to visual splendor.

The animation captures not just the physical elements of the story but also the emotions and expressions of the characters. The use of motion capture technology allows for nuanced performances that convey the wonder, awe, and joy experienced by Hero Boy and his fellow passengers. The characters move with a fluidity and expressiveness that brings them to life, enhancing the overall sense of immersion.

The film's visual splendor extends to the iconic scenes, such as the heart-pounding train ride or the breathtaking moment when the train arrives at the North Pole. These sequences are not just feats of animation but carefully crafted experiences that elicit a sense of childlike wonder, inviting audiences to believe in the extraordinary possibilities of the season.

Belief and the Magic of Christmas:

Central to the narrative of "The Polar Express" is the theme of belief—the belief in the magic of Christmas, the belief in the unseen, and the belief in the power of imagination. The film celebrates the childlike quality of unwavering belief that defines the holiday season for many.

Hero Boy's journey begins with a wavering sense of belief, mirroring the doubts that can creep into the hearts of those who grow older. However, as the story unfolds and he encounters the mystical aspects of the Polar Express, including a train conductor who seems to know his innermost thoughts and a mysterious ghostly hobo, his skepticism gives way to a renewed sense of wonder.

The film beautifully captures the transformative power of belief, illustrating that the magic of Christmas is not confined to the tangible and observable. It exists in the intangible realm of emotions, dreams, and the collective spirit of those who embrace the enchantment of the season. "The Polar Express" encourages viewers to suspend disbelief and rediscover the joy of believing in something beyond the ordinary—a sentiment that resonates with the child in all of us.

Magical Realism and Everyday Magic:

In crafting the world of "The Polar Express," Zemeckis and his team achieved a delicate balance between magical realism and the familiar elements of everyday life. The film seamlessly blends fantastical elements, such as a train that travels to the North Pole and a workshop where elves prepare gifts, with the recognizable settings of a suburban neighborhood and a train station.

This approach contributes to the sense of childlike wonder by suggesting that the extraordinary can exist within the ordinary. The film invites audiences to view the world through the eyes of a child, where even the most mundane surroundings can become imbued with magic and possibility. The juxtaposition of the fantastic and the familiar reinforces the idea that the magic of Christmas is not confined to distant, unreachable realms but is present in the very fabric of our everyday lives.

The film's use of magical realism extends to the interactions with iconic holiday figures, including Santa Claus himself. The portrayal of Santa as a larger-than-life, benevolent figure, complete with a majestic sleigh and a workshop filled with elves, adds to the film's sense of wonder. These fantastical elements coexist with the genuine emotions and experiences of the characters, creating a narrative that feels both timeless and relatable.

Music and Emotional Resonance:

The musical score of "The Polar Express" plays a pivotal role in evoking a sense of childlike wonder. Composed by Alan Silvestri, the music complements the visuals and narrative, enhancing the emotional resonance of key moments. From the joyous melodies that accompany the exhilarating train ride to the poignant notes that underscore moments of reflection and belief, the soundtrack becomes a powerful catalyst for the film's emotional impact.

One standout musical sequence is the performance of "Believe" by Josh Groban, a song that encapsulates the film's central theme of belief in the magic of Christmas. The lyrics and melody capture the essence of childlike wonder, encouraging listeners to embrace the spirit of the season with open hearts and unwavering belief. The integration of music as a storytelling device enhances the film's ability to connect with audiences on an emotional level, fostering a sense of wonder that goes beyond the visual narrative.

The Train as a Symbol of Imagination:

The Polar Express itself serves as a symbolic representation of the boundless power of imagination. The train becomes a vessel that transcends the physical constraints of reality, carrying passengers on a journey that defies logic and invites them to experience the extraordinary. The train's ability to traverse mountains, cross icy landscapes, and arrive at the fantastical North Pole becomes a metaphor for the limitless possibilities that exist when one embraces the wonders of imagination.

The train is more than a mode of transportation; it is a conduit for the characters to access a realm where the magic of Christmas becomes tangible. The film encourages viewers to see the train not merely as a conveyance but as a magical gateway to the enchanting and whimsical aspects of the holiday season. In doing so, "The Polar Express" celebrates the timeless connection between trains and the sense of adventure and discovery that captivates the imaginations of children and adults alike.

Cinematic Spectacle and Iconic Imagery:

"The Polar Express" achieves a sense of childlike wonder through its cinematic spectacle and the creation of iconic imagery. The film's visuals, from the cascading mountains of presents at the North Pole to the ethereal Northern Lights, are designed to evoke a sense of awe and captivation. These images become indelible moments that linger in the minds of viewers, creating a visual tapestry that contributes to the film's lasting impact.

Iconic imagery, such as the bell from Santa's sleigh, becomes a symbol of the enduring magic of Christmas. The bell serves as a tangible representation of belief, and its enchanting sound becomes a touchstone for Hero Boy and audiences alike. By creating these visually striking and emotionally resonant images, "The Polar Express" becomes more than a film; it transforms into a cinematic experience that leaves an imprint on the collective memory of those who embark on its magical journey.

The Timeless Appeal of Childhood Wonder:

"The Polar Express" resonates not only because of its captivating narrative and technological achievements but also because it taps into the timeless appeal of childhood wonder. The film invites viewers to reconnect with the sense of magic and excitement that defines the early years of life, when the world is a place of endless possibilities and every day holds the potential for extraordinary discoveries.

By capturing this essence of childhood wonder, "The Polar Express" becomes a film that transcends generational boundaries. It is a cinematic celebration of the universal emotions associated with the holiday season—joy, anticipation, and the unbridled belief in the miraculous. In doing so, the film becomes a cherished tradition, inviting audiences to revisit its enchanting world year after year and pass on the magic to new generations.

Conclusion:

In the realm of holiday cinema, "The Polar Express" stands as a testament to the enduring power of childlike wonder. Through its immersive storytelling, breathtaking animation, and the evocation of universal themes, the film captures the magic of Christmas in a way that transcends age and time. From the moment the train's whistle blows to the climactic encounter with Santa Claus, "The Polar Express" invites audiences to embark on a journey that rekindles the sense of awe and enchantment that defines the holiday season.

As the film's iconic imagery and heartfelt moments continue to resonate with viewers, "The Polar Express" remains a timeless classic—a cinematic sleigh ride that carries us back to the wonder of our childhood and the boundless magic of Christmas. Whether experienced for the first time or revisited as a cherished tradition, the film invites us to believe in the extraordinary, embrace the joy of the season, and rediscover the childlike wonder that makes the holidays truly magical.

Immersive Musical Identity

"The Polar Express" isn't just a visual marvel; it's a symphony of sound that weaves its own magical spell throughout the film. From the moment the first notes of the iconic theme start playing, the audience is enveloped in an immersive musical experience that becomes an integral part of the film's identity. The score, composed by Alan Silvestri, not only enhances the narrative but also serves as a powerful emotional catalyst, contributing to the overall enchantment of this holiday classic.

The Power of Musical Storytelling:

Music has a unique ability to convey emotions, evoke memories, and enhance storytelling, and in "The Polar Express," Alan Silvestri masterfully exploits this power to create a musical tapestry that complements and elevates the film's narrative. The score becomes a character in itself, guiding the emotional journey of the audience and accentuating the magical moments that unfold on screen.

Theme of Belief:

Central to "The Polar Express" is the theme of belief, and Silvestri's score becomes the melodic embodiment of this central idea. The main theme, often referred to as "Believe," captures the essence of the film's narrative. Its uplifting and resonant melody serves as an anthem for the characters' journey and reinforces the overarching message of the story— that the magic of Christmas is real for those who believe.

The orchestral arrangement, featuring a prominent use of strings and a choir, creates a sense of grandeur and warmth.

The swelling crescendos mirror the characters' emotional arcs, reaching peaks during moments of revelation and belief. Silvestri's ability to infuse the score with a sense of wonder aligns perfectly with the film's exploration of the extraordinary in the ordinary.

Scoring the Journey:

"The Polar Express" is a film that thrives on its journey, both literal and metaphorical, and the score serves as the musical companion guiding audiences through the various stages of this enchanting adventure. From the initial excitement of the train's arrival to the suspenseful moments during the train ride and the ultimate revelation at the North Pole, Silvestri's compositions heighten the sensory experience.

The playful use of instruments, including bells and chimes, contributes to the whimsical atmosphere of the film. These musical elements not only accompany the visual spectacle but also become integral to the storytelling. The score effectively captures the rhythm of the train wheels, the jingling of sleigh bells, and the magical soundscape of the North Pole, creating a multisensory experience that immerses audiences in the world of "The Polar Express."

Emotional Resonance:

Silvestri's ability to evoke deep emotional resonance is particularly evident in the quieter moments of the film. The delicate piano melodies and gentle strings underscore moments of reflection, introspection, and connection. These subtle musical choices enhance the emotional weight of key scenes, allowing the audience to connect with the characters on a profound level.

For instance, during the poignant scene where the young Hero Boy receives the first gift of Christmas, the score takes on a tender and emotive quality. The music communicates the significance of this moment not just as a plot point but as a testament to the transformative power of selflessness and generosity. Silvestri's score becomes a conduit for the emotional impact of the narrative, transcending the boundaries of dialogue and visuals.

The Allure of Christmas Classics:

Part of what makes a Christmas movie enduring is its ability to become a perennial classic, and a memorable musical score is often a key contributor to that status. The best Christmas movies are those that become synonymous with the holiday season, and their music becomes ingrained in the collective memory of audiences.

"The Polar Express" achieves this by not only incorporating original compositions but also by reimagining classic holiday tunes. The film seamlessly weaves familiar melodies into its score, creating a musical landscape that pays homage to the rich tradition of Christmas music. Whether it's the cheerful rendition of "Winter Wonderland" during the joyful arrival at the North Pole or the heartwarming performance of "Believe" by Josh Groban, these musical choices connect "The Polar Express" to the broader tapestry of beloved holiday classics.

Josh Groban's "Believe":

One standout moment in the film's musical identity is the inclusion of "Believe," performed by acclaimed singer Josh Groban. This original song, written by Glen Ballard and Alan Silvestri, serves as both a thematic centerpiece and a standalone anthem for the film. Groban's soulful and evocative vocals bring an additional layer of emotion to the already powerful lyrics.

"Believe" encapsulates the film's core message—that the magic of Christmas is real for those who hold onto their belief. Groban's delivery infuses the song with sincerity and conviction, making it a timeless addition to the soundtrack. The song's impact extends beyond the film, becoming a standalone holiday classic that resonates with audiences during the festive season.

Musical Symbolism:

Silvestri's score is rich with musical symbolism that enhances the thematic elements of the film. The use of recurring motifs, musical themes associated with specific characters or moments, adds a layer of cohesion to the score. For example, the motif associated with the mysterious hobo on the train carries a sense of intrigue and otherworldliness, enriching the character's enigmatic presence.

Additionally, the choice of instruments, such as the use of a choir during key moments, amplifies the film's spiritual and transcendent themes. The choir becomes a vocal representation of the unseen wonders of Christmas, heightening the sense of awe and reverence.

The Role of Sound Design:

Beyond the musical score, the film's sound design plays a crucial role in creating an immersive auditory experience. The meticulously crafted sound effects, from the rhythmic chugging of the train to the rustling of the wind, contribute to the overall sensory immersion. The marriage of the musical score with sound design ensures that every auditory element aligns seamlessly with the film's visual and narrative elements.

For instance, the use of bells becomes a recurring motif not only in the score but also in the diegetic sound of the train's bell and the sleigh bells associated with Santa Claus. This continuity of sound enhances the film's thematic consistency and reinforces the magical atmosphere.

Legacy and Cultural Impact:

"The Polar Express" has not only become a beloved Christmas film but has left an indelible mark on the cultural landscape. Much of its enduring appeal can be attributed to the film's immersive musical identity. The score, with its evocative themes and memorable melodies, has become synonymous with the magic of Christmas for audiences around the world.

Each holiday season, as families gather to watch "The Polar Express," the soundtrack becomes a familiar and cherished companion. The melodies trigger a sense of nostalgia, transporting viewers back to the first time they experienced the film's enchanting world. The enduring popularity of the film and its music ensures that it will continue to be a part of holiday traditions for generations to come.

Conclusion:

In the realm of holiday cinema, "The Polar Express" stands out not only for its groundbreaking animation and heartwarming narrative but also for its immersive musical identity. Alan Silvestri's score, along with the inclusion of classic and original songs, elevates the film to a level where the auditory experience becomes as enchanting as the visual one.

"The Polar Express" reminds us that a truly magical cinematic experience extends beyond what we see on screen—it encompasses what we hear and feel. The film's musical identity, with its emotional resonance, thematic richness, and cultural significance, ensures that it will continue to be a cherished part of the holiday season, enchanting audiences and inspiring belief in the magic of Christmas for years to come.

"The Polar Express" is a film that has elicited a wide spectrum of responses from critics since its release in 2004. While many audiences have embraced it as a heartwarming and visually stunning holiday classic, critics have presented a diverse range of opinions, sparking discussions about the film's merits, its animation style, and its place in the pantheon of Christmas cinema.

Pioneering Animation Techniques:

One aspect of "The Polar Express" that drew immediate attention, both positive and negative, was its pioneering use of motion capture technology. Directed by Robert Zemeckis, the film marked a departure from traditional animation methods, opting instead for a process that involved capturing the movements and expressions of live actors and translating them into digital characters.

Proponents of this innovative approach praised it for pushing the boundaries of what animation could achieve. The lifelike movements of the characters, the intricate details in facial expressions, and the seamless integration of live-action elements with animation were heralded as groundbreaking achievements. The film's use of motion capture was seen as a leap forward in animation technology, offering a new way to bring stories to life on the big screen.

However, not all critics were enamored with this departure from traditional animation. Some expressed reservations about the film's characters falling into the uncanny valley—a term used to describe the unsettling feeling when animated characters appear almost but not quite realistic. The quest for lifelike depictions resulted in characters that some found slightly eerie, raising questions about the limitations and potential pitfalls of motion capture technology.

Narrative Simplicity vs. Emotional Depth:

Critics also diverged in their assessments of the film's narrative. "The Polar Express" is, at its core, a simple and timeless story about the power of belief and the magic of Christmas. For some, this simplicity was a strength, allowing the film to capture the essence of childhood wonder and deliver a message that resonated across generations.

The film's narrative structure, centered around a young boy's journey on a magical train to the North Pole, drew comparisons to classic children's literature. The episodic nature of the journey, with its encounters with various characters and challenges, echoed the structure of beloved adventure stories. Proponents of this approach argued that the film successfully tapped into the universal appeal of timeless tales, creating a narrative that could be embraced by viewers of all ages.

Conversely, some critics contended that the film's simplicity bordered on predictability. The straightforward plot and the adherence to certain tropes of holiday storytelling were viewed by some as lacking the depth and complexity found in other animated classics. While the film aimed to capture the spirit of childhood, some critics questioned whether it offered enough substance to engage adult audiences on a deeper emotional level.

Visual Splendor vs. Lack of Artistic Variation:

The visual design of "The Polar Express" has been both lauded and criticized. The film's portrayal of the North Pole, the interior of the train, and the wintry landscapes received acclaim for their visual splendor. The use of motion capture allowed for detailed and expressive characters, and the film's attention to visual spectacle contributed to its status as a holiday extravaganza.

However, some critics argued that the film's commitment to realism resulted in a lack of variation in its artistic style. The characters, while technically impressive, were seen by some as lacking the distinct visual flair found in other animated films. The film's dedication to achieving a lifelike aesthetic left little room for the exaggerated expressions and stylized character designs that often define the animated medium.

Additionally, the film's reliance on a muted color palette, predominantly featuring whites and blues to evoke a winter atmosphere, was viewed by some as limiting the visual dynamism. While the intention was to create a cohesive and atmospheric world, critics pointed out that the film's visuals might lack the vibrancy found in other holiday classics.

Music as a Divisive Element:

The film's musical identity, celebrated by many, also became a point of contention among critics. Alan Silvestri's score, particularly the main theme "Believe," received praise for its emotional resonance and thematic significance. The integration of classic and original songs, including the standout performance of "Believe" by Josh Groban, contributed to the film's immersive auditory experience.

However, some critics argued that the film's reliance on musical sequences, particularly the performance of "Believe," bordered on sentimentality. The emotional weight conveyed through the music was seen by some as an attempt to compensate for perceived shortcomings in the narrative. While supporters lauded the musical elements for enhancing the emotional impact of key scenes, detractors contended that the film might have relied too heavily on its musical components to elicit a specific emotional response.

Audience Reception vs. Critical Evaluation:

One intriguing aspect of "The Polar Express" is the stark contrast between critical evaluations and audience reception. While some critics raised concerns about the film's animation style, narrative simplicity, and visual choices, audiences embraced it wholeheartedly. The film has become a staple of holiday traditions for many families, with its annual broadcast and home-viewing sessions contributing to its enduring popularity.

Audiences, particularly younger viewers, were captivated by the film's magical world, the sense of adventure, and the overarching themes of belief and wonder. The immersive experience of watching "The Polar Express" during the holiday season became a cherished tradition for many, transcending any critical reservations.

This divergence between critical assessments and audience love highlights the subjective nature of film appreciation. While critics analyze films through a lens of artistic merit, storytelling, and technical proficiency, audiences often connect with films on a more emotional and personal level. "The Polar Express" has, in many ways, become a testament to the power of cinematic experiences that resonate with the hearts and imaginations of viewers.

Legacy and Continued Discussion:

As "The Polar Express" has aged, its place in the realm of Christmas classics has solidified. The film's mixed critical reception has not diminished its cultural impact or its standing as a beloved holiday film. It continues to be celebrated by audiences worldwide, and its influence is evident in the countless discussions, reviews, and analyses that resurface each holiday season.

The film's legacy invites ongoing conversations about the intersection of technology and storytelling in animation, the balance between visual realism and artistic expression, and the enduring appeal of simple yet profound narratives. While critics may continue to offer varied perspectives on "The Polar Express," its enduring popularity suggests that, ultimately, the magic it brings to audiences transcends any critical scrutiny.

Conclusion:

"The Polar Express" stands as a film that elicits diverse reactions, sparking conversations about animation techniques, narrative choices, and the intersection of critical evaluation with audience reception. While critics have presented a spectrum of opinions, the film's enduring popularity and status as a holiday classic underscore the subjective nature of cinematic appreciation.

The discussions surrounding "The Polar Express" serve as a testament to the film's ability to provoke thought, inspire nostalgia, and generate ongoing dialogue about what defines a beloved Christmas movie. As audiences continue to embark on the magical journey of "The Polar Express" each holiday season, the film remains a captivating and enchanting experience that invites viewers to believe in the extraordinary, despite any critical reservations.

Chapter 9 - National Lampoon's Christmas Vacation (1989)

Over-the-Top Slapstick

"National Lampoon's Christmas Vacation" stands as a comedic beacon in the realm of holiday films, renowned for its irreverent humor and over-the-top slapstick antics. Directed by Jeremiah S. Chechik and written by John Hughes, the film takes the Griswold family, led by the hapless Clark Griswold (played by Chevy Chase), through a chaotic and calamitous Christmas celebration. At the heart of its comedic brilliance lies a dedication to over-the-top slapstick, a comedic style that embraces exaggeration, physical comedy, and absurdity to elicit laughter.

Setting the Stage for Hilarity:

The film wastes no time setting the stage for its brand of humor. From the very beginning, as Clark Griswold embarks on a quest to find the perfect Christmas tree, the audience is thrust into a world where reality is stretched to its comedic limits. The exaggerated nature of Clark's determination and the absurdly large tree he ultimately chooses serve as a harbinger of the slapstick chaos that will unfold throughout the film.

Slapstick, in its purest form, relies on physical comedy, sight gags, and absurd situations to generate laughs. "Christmas Vacation" takes these elements and amplifies them, creating a comedic atmosphere where no sight gag is too outlandish, and no physical mishap is too extreme. The film embraces a philosophy of "bigger is funnier," pushing the boundaries of realism to deliver a relentless onslaught of laughs.

The Art of Physical Comedy:

At the core of over-the-top slapstick is the art of physical comedy, and "Christmas Vacation" masterfully employs this comedic technique. Chevy Chase's portrayal of Clark Griswold becomes a canvas for physical humor, with Chase using his facial expressions, body language, and impeccable timing to elicit laughs without uttering a word. The film revels in the misadventures and pratfalls of its characters, turning ordinary situations into opportunities for outrageous physical comedy.

For instance, the iconic scene involving Clark's attempt to install Christmas lights on the house becomes a symphony of slapstick. From the precarious positioning on the roof to the multiple failed attempts at getting the lights to work, each misstep and mishap is exaggerated for comedic effect. The escalation of physical comedy in this scene, culminating in a chaotic explosion of Christmas lights, epitomizes the film's commitment to over-the-top hilarity.

Clark Griswold's Everyman Absurdity:

One of the reasons the over-the-top slapstick works so effectively in "Christmas Vacation" is the relatability of Clark Griswold as an everyman character. While the situations he finds himself in are exaggerated for comedic effect, the essence of his character—the well-intentioned but perpetually bumbling father—resonates with audiences. The absurdity of his predicaments becomes an extension of the universal struggles and mishaps that many individuals experience during the holiday season.

Clark's attempts to create the perfect Christmas for his family, despite constant setbacks, mirror the real-life challenges and absurdities of holiday preparations. The exaggeration of these challenges amplifies the humor, allowing audiences to laugh not only at the fictional misfortunes of the Griswold family but also at the recognition of similar moments in their own lives.

Rube Goldberg-esque Escalation:

A hallmark of over-the-top slapstick is the Rube Goldberg-esque escalation of comedic situations. The film thrives on the principle that if something can go wrong, it will, and in the most spectacular and absurd manner possible. Each misfortune that befalls the Griswold family sets off a chain reaction of events, leading to increasingly chaotic and hilarious outcomes.

Take, for example, the scene involving Uncle Lewis (played by William Hickey) and Aunt Bethany (played by Mae Questel) arriving for Christmas dinner. The seemingly simple act of welcoming guests spirals into a series of absurd events, including a cat getting electrocuted, a Christmas tree catching fire, and the turkey exploding. The escalating absurdity in this sequence is a quintessential example of over-the-top slapstick, with each event more outrageous than the last.

Visual Gags and Absurdity:

In addition to physical comedy, "Christmas Vacation" relies heavily on visual gags and absurd situations to elicit laughter. The film embraces the principle that the more visually absurd and unexpected a situation is, the funnier it becomes.

From the Griswold family's disastrous attempt at sledding to the chaotic Christmas dinner, the film presents a series of comedic tableaus that border on the surreal.

One notable visual gag is the infamous scene involving Clark's daydream about his ideal Christmas bonus. The over-the-top fantasy sequence, complete with a pool full of money and a scantily clad woman, serves as a satirical commentary on the exaggerated expectations and materialism associated with the holiday season. The visual absurdity of this sequence adds a layer of social commentary to the film's comedic arsenal.

Cultural Commentary through Comedy:

While "Christmas Vacation" is primarily a comedy, it doesn't shy away from incorporating elements of cultural commentary. The film uses its over-the-top slapstick style to satirize societal expectations, consumerism, and the pressure to create the perfect holiday experience. The Griswold family becomes a caricatured representation of the challenges and absurdities associated with the commercialized version of Christmas.

By exaggerating these cultural elements, the film invites audiences to reflect on the inherent silliness and stress of conforming to societal expectations during the holidays. The over-the-top nature of the comedy serves as a vehicle for the film to poke fun at the excesses and contradictions of the season while delivering belly laughs.

Chevy Chase's Physical Comedy Prowess:

A significant contributor to the success of the over-the-top slapstick in "Christmas Vacation" is the comedic prowess of

Chevy Chase. Chase's background in physical comedy, honed during his time on "Saturday Night Live," is on full display in the film. His ability to execute precise physical gags, facial expressions, and pratfalls elevates the humor, turning Clark Griswold into an iconic comedic character.

Chase's performance embodies the spirit of the over-the-top slapstick genre, where the physicality of the actor becomes an integral part of the humor. Whether it's Clark's exaggerated reactions to calamities or his signature pratfalls, Chase's comedic timing and commitment to the physical aspects of the role contribute significantly to the film's enduring comedic legacy.

Audience Response and Enduring Popularity:

The success of "Christmas Vacation" lies not only in its dedication to over-the-top slapstick but also in its ability to connect with audiences on a visceral and comedic level. The film's unapologetic embrace of absurdity and chaos resonates with viewers, making it a go-to holiday comedy for generations.

Audiences have embraced the Griswold family's misadventures as a humorous reflection of the challenges and absurdities inherent in the holiday season. The film's slapstick sensibilities, paired with memorable visual gags and Chevy Chase's comedic genius, create a perfect storm of laughter that transcends generational boundaries.

Conclusion:

"National Lampoon's Christmas Vacation" stands as a testament to the enduring appeal of over-the-top slapstick in holiday cinema. The film's dedication to exaggerated physical comedy, visual absurdity, and cultural satire has solidified its place as a beloved Christmas classic. Through the misadventures of the Griswold family, the film invites audiences to embrace the chaos and absurdity of the holiday season with laughter—a tradition that continues to bring joy to viewers year after year.

"National Lampoon's Christmas Vacation" isn't just a slapstick comedy; it's a mirror reflecting the relatable and sometimes tumultuous nature of family gatherings during the holiday season. In its exploration of the Griswold family's Christmas festivities, the film delves into the chaotic, frustrating, and heartwarming aspects of bringing family members together for the holidays. Through a lens of humor and exaggeration, "Christmas Vacation" manages to capture the essence of relatable family gathering struggles that resonate with audiences year after year.

The Myth of the Perfect Christmas:

One of the central themes explored in "Christmas Vacation" is the pursuit of the mythical "perfect Christmas." Clark Griswold, embodying the archetype of the well-meaning but perpetually optimistic patriarch, dreams of creating an idyllic holiday experience for his family. This pursuit, fueled by societal expectations and a desire for a picture-perfect celebration, becomes a relatable struggle for many viewers.

The pressure to live up to the idealized image of Christmas, often perpetuated by media, advertising, and cultural norms, is a universal experience. Families, in their attempt to recreate the magic of the season, often find themselves grappling with unrealistic expectations and the inevitable gap between the fantasy of a flawless holiday and the messy reality of family life.

Navigating Family Dynamics:

"Christmas Vacation" excels in portraying the dynamics of extended family interactions during the holidays. The arrival of relatives, each with their unique quirks and idiosyncrasies, sets the stage for comedic clashes and relatable moments. The film tackles the challenges of navigating family dynamics with humor, highlighting the inherent tensions and joys that come with bringing diverse personalities together under one roof.

Uncle Lewis and Aunt Bethany, two eccentric relatives, embody the type of characters often found in extended families. Their presence adds a layer of absurdity to the family gathering, but it also reflects the unpredictable nature of holiday reunions. Viewers may find echoes of their own family members in these characters, recognizing the blend of eccentricity and endearing qualities that often define family relationships.

The Challenge of Expectations vs. Reality:

"Christmas Vacation" cleverly plays with the dichotomy between expectations and reality, a theme that resonates with anyone who has experienced the highs and lows of holiday preparations. From Clark's ambitious plans for the outdoor Christmas lights display to the anticipation of a generous Christmas bonus, the film showcases the often comical disparity between what we envision for the holidays and the unpredictable reality that unfolds.

The struggle to align expectations with reality is a central theme that viewers find relatable. The film acknowledges the frustration that can arise when meticulous plans go awry, whether it's due to malfunctioning Christmas lights, an unexpected visit from the in-laws, or the perennial challenge of managing family members' differing opinions and preferences. By portraying these struggles with humor, "Christmas Vacation" invites viewers to laugh at the absurdity of the pursuit of holiday perfection.

The Relentless Pursuit of Traditions:

Traditions play a significant role in shaping the holiday experience, and "Christmas Vacation" explores the lengths to which families go to uphold and create their own traditions. Clark Griswold's determination to provide the perfect Christmas, rooted in his own childhood memories and traditions, becomes a driving force that propels the narrative.

The film satirizes the relentless pursuit of traditions, highlighting both the endearing and absurd aspects of this aspect of the holiday season. Whether it's the meticulous planning of the Christmas dinner or the dedication to finding the ideal tree, the Griswold family's commitment to traditions mirrors the rituals and customs that families often hold dear, even when faced with the comedic challenges that arise.

The Role of Miscommunication:

"Christmas Vacation" humorously tackles the theme of miscommunication, a common source of tension in family gatherings. From misunderstandings about the arrival of guests to Clark's misinterpretation of his employer's intentions regarding Christmas bonuses, the film illustrates how miscommunication can lead to chaotic and often hilarious outcomes.

The Griswold family's misadventures serve as a comedic exaggeration of the communication breakdowns that can occur during the holiday season. Viewers may recognize the familiar scenarios of crossed wires, missed signals, and the chaos that ensues when family members aren't on the same page. Through humor, the film highlights the importance of clear communication in avoiding misunderstandings and preventing holiday mishaps.

Sibling Rivalry and Generational Differences:

The portrayal of sibling dynamics and generational differences adds another layer of relatability to "Christmas Vacation." The arrival of Clark's in-laws introduces a clash of generational perspectives, with the older generation often expressing bewilderment at the unconventional choices and modern conveniences embraced by the Griswold family.

The tensions between Clark and his yuppie neighbor, Todd Chester, also touch on the theme of sibling rivalry and the desire to outdo one another in the realm of holiday decorations. This rivalry, while exaggerated for comedic effect, reflects the competitive spirit that can arise between neighbors or even family members during the holiday season. It's a humorous take on the sometimes absurd lengths to which individuals may go to prove the superiority of their holiday celebrations.

The Stress of Hosting:

Hosting family gatherings during the holidays comes with its own set of challenges, and "Christmas Vacation" doesn't shy away from portraying the stress that can accompany playing the role of the host. From preparing elaborate meals to ensuring the comfort of guests, the film captures the chaos and comedic mishaps that unfold when the responsibility of hosting falls on one individual.

The stress of hosting is a relatable aspect of the holiday experience. Whether it's dealing with unexpected guests, culinary disasters, or the pressure to create a festive atmosphere, viewers may empathize with Clark Griswold's increasingly frantic attempts to maintain control over the situation. Through humor, the film provides a cathartic release for those who have navigated the challenges of being the holiday host.

The Unpredictability of Family:

"Christmas Vacation" embraces the unpredictability of family life, recognizing that, despite our best-laid plans, the unexpected is bound to happen. The film revels in the chaos that ensues when family members come together, each with their own agendas, personalities, and baggage. It's a celebration of the messy, imperfect, and ultimately endearing nature of familial relationships.

While the Griswold family's experiences may be exaggerated for comedic effect, the core of their struggles resonates with viewers who have navigated the unpredictable terrain of family gatherings. The film becomes a comedic commentary on the unpredictability of family dynamics, emphasizing that, despite the challenges, the shared moments of laughter, frustration, and connection are what make the holiday season memorable.

The Importance of Togetherness:

Beneath the comedic chaos and relatable struggles, "Christmas Vacation" carries a heartfelt message about the importance of togetherness during the holidays. Despite the mishaps, misunderstandings, and absurdities, the Griswold family ultimately comes together to celebrate Christmas. The film suggests that, beyond the pursuit of perfection and the challenges of family dynamics, the shared moments of joy and connection are what truly define the holiday spirit.

The closing scenes of the film, where the Griswold family gathers around the Christmas tree, exemplify the enduring theme of togetherness. The chaotic journey becomes a shared memory, reinforcing the idea that, in the end, it's the presence of loved ones that makes the holiday season special.

Conclusion:

"Christmas Vacation" succeeds not only as a slapstick comedy but as a relatable exploration of the struggles and joys associated with family gatherings during the holidays. Through humor and exaggeration, the film captures the essence of the human experience—the pursuit of perfection, the challenges of communication, and the enduring importance of togetherness. As viewers laugh along with the Griswold family's misadventures, they find echoes of their own experiences, making "Christmas Vacation" a timeless and beloved portrayal of the relatable struggles that define the holiday season.

"National Lampoon's Christmas Vacation" isn't just a holiday comedy; it's a cultural phenomenon that has left an indelible mark on popular culture. Since its release in 1989, the film has become a staple of the holiday season, cherished for its humor, relatability, and memorable moments. In this exploration of "Christmas Vacation's" lasting pop culture impact, we delve into the elements that have elevated the film beyond a mere Christmas movie, turning it into a timeless and iconic part of the festive landscape.

The Quotable Dialogue:

One of the defining features that cements "Christmas Vacation's" place in pop culture is its endlessly quotable dialogue. Written by John Hughes, the script is a treasure trove of memorable lines and exchanges that have become embedded in the lexicon of holiday conversations. From Clark Griswold's enthusiastic yet exasperated declarations to Cousin Eddie's eccentric and unforgettable remarks, the film's dialogue has transcended its cinematic origins to become part of the cultural fabric.

Lines such as "It's the gift that keeps on giving the whole year," "Shitter's full," and "Hallelujah! Holy [expletive]! Where's the Tylenol?" have become shorthand for expressing holiday sentiments and capturing the comedic essence of "Christmas Vacation." These quotes are not just lines from a movie; they've become communal expressions of the shared experiences and frustrations that accompany the holiday season.

The Iconic Imagery:

"Christmas Vacation" is replete with iconic imagery that has become synonymous with the holiday season. The image of Clark Griswold standing proudly in front of his house adorned with an excessive number of Christmas lights has become a symbol of both festive enthusiasm and the pursuit of the perfect holiday display. This image, often replicated and parodied, encapsulates the film's theme of the relentless quest for the idealized Christmas experience.

Similarly, the Griswold family Christmas tree, a behemoth that barely fits into the living room, serves as a visual metaphor for the larger-than-life aspirations and challenges of holiday traditions. The image of the tree, adorned with an abundance of decorations and teetering precariously, captures the film's blend of humor and sentimentality.

Additionally, the recurring visual motif of Clark's fantasies—most notably, his daydream about receiving a lavish Christmas bonus—has become an iconic representation of the holiday season's materialistic expectations. These images have not only endured in the context of the film but have been repurposed and referenced in various forms of media, solidifying their status as cultural touchstones.

Cousin Eddie's Legacy:

Few characters in cinematic history have left as lasting an impression as Cousin Eddie, played by Randy Quaid. Eddie's eccentricities, outlandish behavior, and memorable one-liners have elevated him to the status of a cultural icon. The character's unkempt appearance, adorned in a white bathrobe and a trooper hat, has become synonymous with the archetype of the quirky and uninvited family member during the holidays.

Cousin Eddie's most famous scene, where he empties his RV's septic tank into the storm drain while wearing a bathrobe and sipping eggnog, has become a legendary moment in comedy history. The character's unpredictable and unfiltered nature resonates with audiences, making Eddie a symbol of the unexpected chaos that can accompany family gatherings.

Eddie's legacy extends beyond "Christmas Vacation" through references in other films, television shows, and even in political discourse. The character's impact is a testament to the enduring appeal of well-crafted comedic personas and their ability to transcend the boundaries of a single film.

Musical Contributions:

"Christmas Vacation" features a memorable musical score that contributes significantly to its enduring popularity. The film's theme song, "Christmas Vacation," performed by Mavis Staples, has become synonymous with the holiday season. The upbeat and festive tune captures the spirit of the film and, by extension, the joyous anticipation of Christmas celebrations.

The soundtrack, featuring both classic holiday tunes and original compositions, complements the film's comedic and heartwarming moments. Songs like "Mele Kalikimaka" during the pool fantasy sequence and the instrumental arrangement of "Here Comes Santa Claus" when Clark finally succeeds in lighting up the house contribute to the film's lasting musical impact.

The use of music in "Christmas Vacation" goes beyond the film itself. The theme song, in particular, has been embraced as a seasonal anthem, played on radio stations and featured in holiday playlists. Its catchy melody and festive lyrics have helped solidify the song's place in the pantheon of Christmas music, adding another layer to the film's enduring cultural legacy.

Homage and Parody in Popular Media:

"Christmas Vacation" has become a source of inspiration for countless homages and parodies in popular media. From television shows and commercials to animated series and internet memes, the film's iconic moments and characters have been repurposed and referenced in a variety of contexts.

Television series like "The Simpsons" and "Saturday Night Live" have paid homage to "Christmas Vacation" through parodying its scenes and characters. The Griswold family's misadventures have become a template for comedic explorations of holiday chaos, resonating with audiences who recognize the familiar tropes presented in the film.

Commercials often draw on the imagery and themes of "Christmas Vacation" to evoke a sense of holiday nostalgia and humor. The characters of Clark Griswold and Cousin Eddie have been featured in advertising campaigns, with actors reprising their roles to capture the essence of the film's humor for promotional purposes.

Internet memes, GIFs, and social media posts regularly reference "Christmas Vacation," using its quotes and scenes to express sentiments related to the holiday season. The film's cultural impact has transcended traditional media, finding new life in the digital age as audiences continue to share and celebrate its comedic moments.

Annual Tradition and Television Broadcasts:

A significant factor in "Christmas Vacation's" enduring popularity is its status as an annual tradition for many families. The film has become a staple of holiday programming, with television networks scheduling regular broadcasts during the Christmas season. The tradition of tuning in to watch the Griswold family's Christmas escapades has become a shared experience for viewers, creating a sense of continuity and nostalgia.

The annual television broadcasts not only introduce the film to new generations but also provide an opportunity for existing fans to revisit the comedic magic of "Christmas Vacation" each year. The film's presence in holiday lineups has solidified its place as a classic, ensuring that its humor and warmth continue to be a part of the festive season for years to come.

Merchandising and Cultural Merchants:

The cultural impact of "Christmas Vacation" is further evident in the extensive merchandising associated with the film. From branded merchandise featuring the Griswold family to themed Christmas ornaments, the film has inspired a wide array of products that capitalize on its enduring popularity.

Christmas sweaters adorned with images of Clark Griswold's illuminated house, action figures depicting the characters, and holiday decorations featuring Cousin Eddie's

RV are just a few examples of the merchandise that allows fans to incorporate "Christmas Vacation" into their own holiday celebrations. The film's characters and iconic moments have become cultural currency, appearing on a range of products that contribute to the film's continued presence in the marketplace.

Legacy of Laughter and Comfort:

Beyond the individual components of its cultural impact, the lasting legacy of "Christmas Vacation" lies in its ability to evoke laughter and provide a sense of comfort during the holiday season. The film's humor, relatability, and timeless themes of family, tradition, and the pursuit of the perfect Christmas experience resonate with audiences year after year.

"Christmas Vacation" has become more than a movie; it's a tradition, a cultural touchstone, and a source of shared joy. Its enduring popularity is a testament to the universal appeal of holiday comedies that capture the essence of the human experience. As long as families gather to celebrate the holidays, the Griswold family's misadventures will continue to be a cherished part of the festive season, bringing laughter and warmth to generations old and new.

Comparison to Other Vacation Movies

"National Lampoon's Christmas Vacation" stands as a unique entry in the Vacation film series, deviating from the typical summer road trip formula that characterized its predecessors. As the third installment in the Vacation franchise, the film distinguishes itself by shifting the Griswold family's comedic misadventures from a summer vacation to the chaotic landscape of the holiday season. In this exploration, we'll delve into how "Christmas Vacation" compares to the other Vacation movies, examining the thematic differences, comedic evolution, and the enduring appeal that sets it apart within the beloved series.

Thematic Shifts and Seasonal Humor:

The Vacation film series, initiated by "National Lampoon's Vacation" in 1983, traditionally centered around the misadventures of the Griswold family during summer vacations. These films, including "European Vacation" (1985) and "Vegas Vacation" (1997), followed a consistent formula of the Griswolds embarking on a road trip, encountering a series of comedic obstacles, and ultimately finding themselves in hilariously absurd situations.

"Christmas Vacation" breaks away from this established formula by shifting the setting to the winter holiday season. This thematic shift allows the film to explore the unique challenges and dynamics associated with Christmas celebrations, introducing a new layer of humor grounded in the traditions, expectations, and chaos inherent to the festive period. The film's exploration of holiday-specific themes, such as the quest for the perfect Christmas and the challenges of family gatherings, distinguishes it from its summer-centric predecessors.

Evolution of Clark Griswold:

One of the defining elements of the Vacation series is the central character, Clark Griswold, portrayed by Chevy Chase. Across the films, Clark evolves from an optimistic and well-meaning family man to a symbol of comedic resilience in the face of absurdity. "Christmas Vacation" showcases a matured and enduring version of Clark, whose relentless pursuit of the perfect holiday experience reflects both growth and the persistence of his characteristic enthusiasm.

In contrast to the earlier films where Clark's goals revolved around creating the ideal family vacation, "Christmas Vacation" sees him channeling that same determination into crafting the perfect Christmas for his family. The evolution of Clark's character adds depth to the film, as audiences witness not only the consistency of his comedic traits but also a relatable progression in his role as a family patriarch navigating the challenges of the holiday season.

Family Dynamics and Traditions:

While the Vacation series has always emphasized the dynamics of the Griswold family, "Christmas Vacation" places a unique spotlight on the intricacies of family gatherings during the holidays. The film explores the challenges and joys associated with hosting relatives, navigating generational differences, and adhering to cherished holiday traditions. These themes, deeply rooted in the Christmas experience, contribute to the film's distinct narrative and comedic dynamics.

Unlike the spontaneous and unpredictable nature of the summer vacations in earlier films, "Christmas Vacation" portrays the Griswold family grappling with the expectations and pressures specific to the holiday season. The portrayal of extended family members, such as the eccentric Cousin Eddie, introduces a new dimension to the family dynamics, emphasizing the blend of chaos and warmth that defines holiday gatherings.

The Quest for the Perfect Christmas:

Throughout the Vacation series, Clark Griswold is characterized by his relentless pursuit of an idealized experience—be it the perfect road trip or, in the case of "Christmas Vacation," the perfect Christmas celebration. The film amplifies this quest, weaving it into the fabric of the holiday narrative. Clark's determination to create a magical Christmas, complete with the grand lighting of the house and a generous Christmas bonus, becomes a central driving force that sets "Christmas Vacation" apart thematically.

The film satirizes the societal and cultural pressures associated with achieving the "perfect" Christmas, presenting a humorous yet relatable commentary on the unrealistic expectations often placed on individuals during the holiday season. This thematic exploration aligns with the overarching narrative of the Vacation series while offering a fresh perspective that resonates specifically with the challenges of Christmas preparations.

Cinematic Style and Visual Humor:

"Christmas Vacation" maintains the comedic visual style established in the earlier Vacation films, characterized by slapstick humor, sight gags, and physical comedy. However, the shift to a winter setting introduces new opportunities for visual humor centered around Christmas traditions. From the chaotic installation of Christmas lights to the precarious journey of the oversized Christmas tree, the film capitalizes on the visual spectacle and absurdity inherent to holiday preparations.

The winter setting also allows for the integration of iconic Christmas imagery, such as the Griswold family's visit to the tree lot and the eventual transformation of the house into a dazzling display of lights. These visual elements contribute to the film's distinct aesthetic, seamlessly blending the comedic style of the Vacation series with the festive charm of Christmas.

Cousin Eddie and Recurring Characters:

"Cousin Eddie," portrayed by Randy Quaid, emerges as a recurring character in the Vacation series, but his role reaches new heights in "Christmas Vacation." Eddie's eccentricities, peculiar mannerisms, and unpredictable behavior become central to the film's comedic dynamics. His unexpected arrival, complete with a dilapidated RV and a host of bizarre antics, adds a layer of absurdity that is uniquely tailored to the holiday setting.

While Eddie's character is introduced in "National Lampoon's Vacation," it's in "Christmas Vacation" that he solidifies his status as an iconic and enduring figure within the series. Eddie's presence, with his distinctive wardrobe and memorable catchphrases, contributes to the film's distinct comedic identity and reinforces the notion that the holiday season brings not only joy but also unexpected and unconventional guests.

Legacy and Cultural Impact:

"Christmas Vacation" has achieved a level of cultural impact and enduring popularity that distinguishes it within the Vacation film series. While the earlier entries in the series hold a special place in comedic cinema history, "Christmas Vacation" stands out as a perennial favorite during the holiday season. Its thematic resonance, seasonal humor, and memorable characters have elevated it to the status of a classic Christmas film, enjoyed by audiences across generations.

The film's legacy extends beyond its initial release, with annual television broadcasts, merchandise, and widespread references in popular media contributing to its enduring popularity. The distinct blend of Vacation-style humor with Christmas themes has created a unique cinematic experience that continues to bring joy and laughter to viewers each holiday season.

Conclusion:

"National Lampoon's Christmas Vacation" not only complements the Vacation film series but also enriches it with a distinctive holiday flavor. The thematic shift to Christmas, the evolution of Clark Griswold, the exploration of family dynamics, and the enduring appeal of characters like Cousin Eddie collectively contribute to the film's unique position within the series. As audiences continue to revisit the misadventures of the Griswold family during the holiday season, "Christmas Vacation" remains a testament to the timeless charm and universal humor that define the Vacation film legacy.

Chapter 10 - The Nightmare Before Christmas (1993) Magic of Stop-Motion Style

Tim Burton's "The Nightmare Before Christmas" is a cinematic masterpiece celebrated for its unique blend of dark fantasy, whimsical characters, and, perhaps most notably, its groundbreaking use of stop-motion animation. In this exploration of the film's "Magic of Stop-Motion Style," we delve into the intricate artistry, technical achievements, and enduring charm that have elevated stop-motion animation to a magical realm, making "The Nightmare Before Christmas" a timeless classic.

The Artistry of Stop-Motion Animation:

Stop-motion animation, a meticulous filmmaking technique that involves capturing individual frames of a physical model in various poses to create movement, has a rich history in the world of cinema. What sets "The Nightmare Before Christmas" apart is not only its commitment to stop-motion but also the unparalleled artistry and craftsmanship that director Henry Selick and his team brought to the process.

Every character in the film, from Jack Skellington to Oogie Boogie, is a tangible, three-dimensional puppet meticulously crafted by skilled animators and artisans. The physicality of these puppets, combined with the painstaking attention to detail in their design, gives "The Nightmare Before Christmas" a tactile and tangible quality that distinguishes it from traditional animated films.

The stop-motion process, involving the precise manipulation of puppets frame by frame, requires an immense level of skill and patience. Animators meticulously move each limb and facial feature to convey the intended emotions and actions. This hands-on approach not only adds a layer of authenticity to the characters but also contributes to the film's overall visual allure.

Expressive Puppets and Character Design:

One of the enchanting aspects of "The Nightmare Before Christmas" is the expressiveness and individuality of each puppet. The character design, led by artist Tim Burton's distinctive vision, embraces a gothic and whimsical aesthetic. Jack Skellington's elongated limbs and expressive skeletal face, Sally's delicately stitched appearance, and the menacing presence of Oogie Boogie—all these characters are brought to life through the artistry of stop-motion animation.

The puppets' facial expressions, despite their often skeletal or fantastical features, convey a remarkable range of emotions. This expressiveness is achieved through the use of replacement heads and facial features that can be swapped between frames. The careful choreography of these facial changes adds depth and nuance to the characters, allowing audiences to empathize with their journeys, fears, and desires.

The physicality of the puppets also plays a crucial role in defining the characters. The way Jack moves with a graceful yet otherworldly elegance or the haphazard and unpredictable movements of Oogie Boogie—all these nuances contribute to the storytelling in a way that goes beyond traditional animation. The tactile nature of the stop-motion puppets enhances the connection between the characters and the audience, creating a sense of intimacy and engagement.

Set Design and Enchanting Worlds:

In addition to the expressive characters, the stop-motion style of "The Nightmare Before Christmas" extends to the enchanting worlds created within the film. The meticulous set design, featuring intricately crafted miniature landscapes, showcases the versatility and imaginative possibilities of stop-motion animation.

The landscapes of Halloween Town, Christmas Town, and other realms within the film are not CGI-generated or drawn on a computer; they are physical sets brought to life by skilled artists and animators. The attention to detail in every cobblestone, twisted tree, and flickering streetlamp contributes to the immersive and fantastical atmosphere of the film.

Stop-motion allows for a tangible and tactile representation of the film's worlds. The use of real materials—whether it's the textured surfaces of buildings or the tangible snow on the ground—adds a layer of authenticity to the film's aesthetic. The painstaking effort to create these physical environments pays off in the visual richness and depth that permeate every frame of "The Nightmare Before Christmas."

The Choreography of Movement:

Stop-motion animation requires a unique form of choreography, where every movement is carefully planned and executed frame by frame. This meticulous approach to movement adds a distinctive rhythm to the characters' actions and interactions, creating a visual language that is both captivating and immersive.

The dance sequences, such as Jack Skellington's iconic "This is Halloween" performance, showcase the fluidity and precision of stop-motion choreography. Each movement is a deliberate pose meticulously crafted to convey the intended emotion or narrative beat. The combination of music, choreography, and stop-motion animation elevates these sequences to a level of artistry that transcends traditional animated filmmaking.

The precision required for stop-motion choreography is a testament to the skill and dedication of the animators. The seamless flow of movement achieved through frame-by-frame manipulation is a defining feature of "The Nightmare Before Christmas," contributing to the film's immersive storytelling and unforgettable visual spectacle.

Technical Innovations and Challenges:

While the artistry of stop-motion animation is central to the film's appeal, the technical innovations and challenges faced by the filmmakers also played a crucial role in shaping the final product. "The Nightmare Before Christmas" pushed the boundaries of what was possible in stop-motion filmmaking, introducing groundbreaking techniques that would influence the industry for years to come.

The film's use of replacement animation, where different facial expressions or body parts are swapped between frames, allowed for a level of expressiveness rarely seen in stop-motion at the time. This technique revolutionized the way characters could convey emotions and interact with their environments, opening new possibilities for storytelling in the medium.

Additionally, the filmmakers employed the use of innovative armatures—a framework within the puppets that allows for precise and controlled movement. These armatures, often made of metal or other durable materials, provided the animators with the necessary stability and control to execute intricate movements with the puppets. The evolution of armature technology in "The Nightmare Before Christmas" set a standard for future stop-motion productions, influencing advancements in the field.

However, these technical innovations also came with significant challenges. The meticulous nature of stop-motion animation requires an immense amount of time and patience. The film's production, spanning several years, involved animators working tirelessly to bring each frame to life. The attention to detail, coupled with the need for consistency in movement and design, made the production of "The Nightmare Before Christmas" an arduous yet groundbreaking endeavor.

Legacy and Influence on Stop-Motion Animation:

"The Nightmare Before Christmas" stands as a landmark film in the history of stop-motion animation, leaving an indelible mark on the industry. Its success not only affirmed the viability of stop-motion as a cinematic art form but also inspired a new generation of animators and filmmakers to explore the possibilities of the medium.

The film's impact on stop-motion animation is evident in the subsequent rise of similarly styled productions.

Filmmakers and studios, inspired by the enchanting worlds and expressive characters of "The Nightmare Before Christmas," began to explore the potential of stop-motion as a storytelling tool. The film's success paved the way for other beloved stop-motion works, such as "Coraline" (2009), "ParaNorman" (2012), and "Kubo and the Two Strings" (2016), which continued to push the boundaries of what could be achieved with the medium.

Additionally, the legacy of "The Nightmare Before Christmas" is visible in the enduring popularity of stop-motion animation in both film and television. The distinctive aesthetic and tactile quality of stop-motion continue to captivate audiences, with new productions embracing the charm and artistry exemplified by Tim Burton's iconic film.

Conclusion:

"The Nightmare Before Christmas" is a testament to the enchanting magic that can be woven through the art of stop-motion animation. The film's meticulous craftsmanship, expressive characters, innovative techniques, and enduring influence have solidified its place as a timeless classic in the realm of animated cinema. As audiences continue to be captivated by the dark yet whimsical world of Jack Skellington and his companions, "The Nightmare Before Christmas" remains a shining example of the unparalleled magic that can be achieved through the stop-motion style.

Score and Musical Numbers

Tim Burton's "The Nightmare Before Christmas" is not merely a visual marvel; it is also a musical masterpiece that weaves its narrative through a hauntingly beautiful score and memorable musical numbers. In this exploration of the film's "Score and Musical Numbers," we delve into the creative brilliance behind the compositions, the thematic resonance of the songs, and the enduring impact of a soundtrack that has become an integral part of the film's identity.

Danny Elfman's Captivating Score:

Central to the musical magic of "The Nightmare Before Christmas" is the evocative and enchanting score composed by the multi-talented Danny Elfman. Elfman, known for his distinctive and eclectic style, crafted a musical landscape that complements the film's dark fantasy while embracing the whimsical nature of its characters and settings.

The score serves as a narrative force, guiding the audience through the film's various moods and themes. From the eerie and mysterious tones that accompany Jack Skellington's explorations to the lively and jubilant melodies of Christmas Town, Elfman's score is a dynamic and integral part of the storytelling process. The music not only enhances the emotional impact of scenes but also establishes a sonic identity that resonates throughout the film.

Elfman's ability to seamlessly blend different musical genres is evident in the score. Elements of Broadway, jazz, classical, and pop are woven together to create a rich and textured musical tapestry. This eclectic approach contributes to the film's timeless quality, ensuring that the soundtrack remains as captivating and innovative today as it was upon the film's release.

Iconic Musical Numbers:

"The Nightmare Before Christmas" is renowned for its standout musical numbers, each of which contributes to the film's narrative and emotional depth. From character solos to ensemble pieces, the songs not only advance the plot but also provide insights into the personalities and motivations of the inhabitants of Halloween Town.

This is Halloween: The film opens with the iconic "This is Halloween," a musical extravaganza that introduces audiences to the ghoulish residents of Halloween Town. With its catchy lyrics, energetic orchestration, and spirited vocal performances, the song sets the stage for the film's dark yet whimsical tone. "This is Halloween" has transcended its role as an introduction and become a cultural phenomenon, often associated with the Halloween season and celebrated for its infectious energy.

Jack's Lament: In "Jack's Lament," Danny Elfman's vocal performance as Jack Skellington captures the character's longing and existential crisis. The melancholic melody and introspective lyrics convey Jack's desire for something more, setting the stage for his journey to discover Christmas Town. The song serves as a pivotal moment in the film, showcasing Elfman's vocal range and the emotional depth that can be conveyed through music.

What's This?: As Jack stumbles upon Christmas Town, "What's This?" emerges as a jubilant celebration of discovery and wonder. Elfman's performance captures Jack's childlike enthusiasm, while the orchestration reflects the magic and enchantment of the holiday season. The juxtaposition of Jack's delight and the bemusement of the Christmas Town residents adds layers of humor and charm to the song.

Sally's Song: "Sally's Song" provides a hauntingly beautiful exploration of Sally's emotions and inner turmoil. The delicate melody and Elfman's emotive delivery convey Sally's sense of longing and her conflicted feelings for Jack. The song adds a poignant layer to the film's romantic subplot, emphasizing the characters' complexity and the challenges they face in navigating their unconventional relationship.

Oogie Boogie's Song: The jazzy and menacing "Oogie Boogie's Song" introduces the film's primary antagonist with theatrical flair. Ken Page's vocal performance as Oogie Boogie exudes a sinister charm, while the upbeat tempo and playful lyrics create a memorable musical moment. The song stands out for its theatricality and showcases Elfman's ability to infuse diverse musical styles into the fabric of the film.

Finale/Reprise: The film's grand finale and reprise bring the narrative full circle, with "Jack's Obsession" and "Poor Jack" reflecting on the consequences of Jack's misguided attempt to take over Christmas. The reprise of "This is Halloween" at the end of the film serves as a bookend, reinforcing the cyclical nature of the holiday worlds. These closing musical moments provide a satisfying resolution to the film's themes while leaving room for interpretation and reflection.

Thematic Resonance and Narrative Integration:

Beyond their melodic appeal, the songs in "The Nightmare Before Christmas" contribute significantly to the film's thematic resonance and narrative cohesion. The music serves as a storytelling device, allowing characters to express their motivations, fears, and desires in a way that complements the visual narrative.

The recurring motif of identity and self-discovery is woven into several musical numbers. Jack's yearning for a sense of purpose in "Jack's Lament," his fascination with Christmas in "What's This?," and Sally's contemplation of her place in the world in "Sally's Song" collectively emphasize the universal themes of identity, longing, and self-realization.

The film's exploration of the collision between Halloween and Christmas is underscored by the contrasting musical styles. The energetic and chaotic rhythms of Halloween Town's songs give way to the joyful and harmonious melodies of Christmas Town, highlighting the clash of these two holiday worlds. The interplay of musical themes mirrors the narrative tension and thematic richness of the film.

The songs also serve as character motifs, providing insight into the personalities and motivations of the inhabitants of Halloween Town. Whether it's the mischievous antics of Lock, Shock, and Barrel in "Kidnap the Sandy Claws" or the sinister allure of Oogie Boogie in his eponymous song, the music becomes an integral part of character development.

Cultural Impact and Enduring Popularity:

The soundtrack of "The Nightmare Before Christmas" has achieved a level of cultural impact that extends far beyond the film itself. The songs have become anthems associated with Halloween and Christmas, transcending the boundaries of the movie and finding a place in popular culture. Covers, parodies, and renditions of the film's songs continue to proliferate, attesting to the enduring popularity of the musical numbers.

The soundtrack's success is also evident in its commercial performance. The album has been reissued multiple times, and the songs have been released as singles, further solidifying their place in the musical landscape. The soundtrack's ability to resonate with audiences across generations speaks to the timeless quality of the music, which remains as enchanting and relevant as it was upon the film's release.

Moreover, the impact of "The Nightmare Before Christmas" on the musical genre in animated films is immeasurable. The film demonstrated that an animated feature could seamlessly integrate music into its storytelling, paving the way for subsequent animated musicals to explore the creative possibilities of combining visuals and music to enhance the narrative.

Conclusion:

"The Nightmare Before Christmas" stands as a testament to the transformative power of music in cinema. Danny Elfman's hauntingly beautiful score and the memorable musical numbers have elevated the film from a visual spectacle to a complete sensory experience. The songs not only contribute to the film's narrative depth and thematic resonance but have also become iconic cultural touchstones, ensuring that the musical legacy of "The Nightmare Before Christmas" continues to enchant and captivate audiences, making it a timeless classic in the realm of animated musicals.

"The Nightmare Before Christmas" is a visual marvel that owes much of its enduring appeal to the iconic and imaginative character designs crafted by a team of skilled artists under the visionary direction of Tim Burton. In this exploration of "Memorable Character Designs," we delve into the distinct visual language of Halloween Town, the intricate details that breathe life into each character, and the lasting impact of a cast that has become synonymous with the film's dark whimsy.

Halloween Town Aesthetic:

At the heart of "The Nightmare Before Christmas" lies Halloween Town, a fantastical realm where every day is Halloween, and the inhabitants are as diverse as they are eerie. The character designs in this macabre yet whimsical world are a testament to the creative genius of Tim Burton and the animators who brought his vision to life.

Jack Skellington: The film's protagonist, Jack Skellington, is an embodiment of Halloween itself. With his skeletal frame, elongated limbs, and distinctive bat bowtie, Jack's design is both iconic and instantly recognizable. His expressive face, despite lacking traditional features, conveys a wide range of emotions, from the joy of discovering Christmas to the existential angst that propels the narrative forward.

Sally: Sally, with her stitched-together appearance and delicate features, is a poignant counterpart to Jack's exuberance. Her design reflects a blend of innocence and resilience, as seen in her large, expressive eyes and the intricate patterns of stitches that adorn her body. The careful detailing of Sally's design extends to her clothing, with the patchwork dress becoming an iconic element of her character.

Oogie Boogie: The primary antagonist, Oogie Boogie, is a masterclass in sinister whimsy. His burlap sack exterior, filled with creepy-crawly creatures, adds a layer of menace to his design. The choice to keep Oogie Boogie in shadow for much of the film heightens the mystery surrounding his character, allowing the audience to focus on the eerie silhouette and the sinister gleam in his glowing eyes.

Lock, Shock, and Barrel: The mischievous trio of Lock, Shock, and Barrel showcase the diversity of character designs in Halloween Town. Each child has a distinct look, from Lock's devilish grin to Shock's witchy attire and Barrel's skeletal mask. Their playful yet slightly menacing designs align perfectly with their roles as Jack's henchmen, adding both charm and mischief to the narrative.

Mayor: The two-faced Mayor of Halloween Town is a literal embodiment of duality, with one face displaying a cheerful expression and the other a perpetual frown. This dual-faced design not only adds a touch of dark humor but also serves as a visual representation of the town's penchant for the bizarre. The Mayor's design reinforces the film's theme of embracing the darker and lighter aspects of existence.

Intricate Details and Artistic Flourishes:

What sets the character designs in "The Nightmare Before Christmas" apart is the attention to detail and the artistic flourishes that breathe life into each inhabitant of

Halloween Town. The use of stop-motion animation allows for a level of craftsmanship that transcends traditional animated characters.

Texture and Tangibility: The tangible and tactile nature of stop-motion animation is evident in the texture of the characters. Jack's bony fingers, Sally's stitched fabric, and Oogie Boogie's sackcloth exterior all possess a palpable quality that adds to the immersive experience of the film. The use of real materials in the puppets, from fabric to clay, contributes to the tactile richness of the character designs.

Expressive Movement: Stop-motion animation allows for precise control over each movement, enabling animators to convey a wide range of emotions through subtle gestures. Jack's graceful movements, Sally's delicate expressions, and the jerky yet playful actions of Lock, Shock, and Barrel all showcase the expressive potential of stop-motion character animation. The careful choreography of movement adds depth to the characters, making them feel alive and dynamic.

Character Transformations: The film features several instances of characters undergoing transformations, and each metamorphosis is a visual spectacle. From Jack's experiments in his laboratory to Sally's daring escapes, the character designs seamlessly adapt to these dynamic changes. The fluidity of these transformations showcases the versatility of stop-motion animation in conveying fantastical and otherworldly elements.

Cultural and Artistic Influences:

The character designs in "The Nightmare Before Christmas" draw inspiration from a variety of cultural and artistic influences, reflecting Tim Burton's eclectic sensibilities. The film's aesthetic is rooted in German Expressionism, a cinematic and artistic movement known for its distorted shapes, chiaroscuro lighting, and surreal landscapes. This influence is particularly evident in the angular and stylized architecture of Halloween Town.

Additionally, Burton's love for the macabre and Gothic is reflected in the character designs. The film pays homage to classic horror films, with characters like the Wolfman, the Mummy, and the Creature from the Black Lagoon making appearances in the Halloween Town population. These nods to horror classics add depth to the film's visual tapestry and showcase Burton's appreciation for cinematic history.

The character designs also echo the quirky and fantastical illustrations found in Burton's own artwork. The exaggerated features, whimsical details, and idiosyncratic charm of the characters align with Burton's signature artistic style, creating a seamless integration between his visual language and the animated world of Halloween Town.

Enduring Appeal and Merchandising Legacy:

The enduring appeal of the character designs in "The Nightmare Before Christmas" is evident in the film's extensive merchandising legacy. The distinctive look of Jack Skellington, Sally, and other characters has transcended the confines of the film, becoming cultural icons with a dedicated fan base.

From action figures to clothing lines, the characters of Halloween Town have found a second life in the world of consumer products. The charm and uniqueness of the character designs make them ideal for adaptation into various forms of merchandise, allowing fans to bring a piece of the film's magic into their everyday lives.

The popularity of "The Nightmare Before Christmas" as a theme in amusement parks, particularly during the Halloween season, further demonstrates the enduring appeal of the character designs. Whether in the form of costumed characters, themed attractions, or merchandise stalls, the characters have become synonymous with the spooky and whimsical atmosphere associated with Halloween celebrations.

Influence on Pop Culture and Animation:

"The Nightmare Before Christmas" has left an indelible mark on pop culture, influencing subsequent animated films and permeating various forms of media. The film's success demonstrated the viability of stop-motion animation as a storytelling medium, paving the way for a resurgence of interest in the technique.

The visual aesthetic of Halloween Town and its inhabitants has inspired countless artists and animators, leading to a wave of creative works that pay homage to the film's distinctive style. The influence of "The Nightmare Before Christmas" is particularly evident in the realm of animated and fantasy films, where the marriage of dark whimsy and fantastical elements has become a sought-after combination.

The film's impact on character design extends beyond the realm of animation. The use of expressive and unconventional character designs has become a hallmark of contemporary animated films, with filmmakers increasingly exploring unique visual styles that break away from traditional norms. "The Nightmare Before Christmas" serves as a testament to the creative possibilities that emerge when filmmakers embrace unconventional and visually striking character designs.

Conclusion:

The character designs in "The Nightmare Before Christmas" stand as a testament to the fusion of artistic vision, craftsmanship, and cultural influences. Each character is a visual masterpiece, embodying the whimsical yet eerie spirit of Halloween Town. The film's enduring appeal is a testament to the iconic nature of these designs, which continue to captivate audiences and inspire artists across generations. As we journey through Halloween Town with Jack, Sally, and the eclectic inhabitants, the character designs serve as a visual symphony, enriching the narrative and ensuring that "The Nightmare Before Christmas" remains a timeless masterpiece in the realm of animated cinema.

Long-Term Fandom and Appeal

"The Nightmare Before Christmas" is not merely a film; it's a cultural phenomenon that has captured the hearts and imaginations of audiences around the world. In this exploration of "Long-Term Fandom and Appeal," we delve into the enduring legacy of the film, the passionate community it has cultivated, and the ways in which it continues to resonate with new generations.

Cultivating a Dedicated Fandom:

Since its release in 1993, "The Nightmare Before Christmas" has cultivated a dedicated and passionate fan base that spans generations. The film's unique blend of dark fantasy, whimsical characters, and memorable music has resonated with viewers of all ages, creating a fandom that transcends traditional demographic boundaries.

Cross-Generational Appeal: One of the remarkable aspects of "The Nightmare Before Christmas" is its ability to appeal to audiences of varying ages. The film's themes of self-discovery, the juxtaposition of darkness and light, and the universal desire for belonging resonate with both children and adults. As a result, parents who grew up with the film are now introducing it to their own children, creating a multi-generational fan base.

Seasonal Traditions: "The Nightmare Before Christmas" has become a staple of seasonal traditions, particularly during Halloween and Christmas. Families and friends often make it a ritual to watch the film together, and its themes aligning with the spirit of both holidays make it a versatile and enduring choice. The film's dual nature, celebrating both Halloween and Christmas, ensures that it remains relevant and beloved throughout the holiday season.

Community Events and Celebrations: Fandom around the film extends beyond individual viewings to community events and celebrations. Many fans participate in themed gatherings, costume parties, and screenings during special occasions. The communal experience of celebrating "The Nightmare Before Christmas" reinforces the sense of belonging within the fandom and contributes to the film's lasting appeal.

Merchandising and Collectibles:

The film's characters and imagery have become synonymous with a wide array of merchandise and collectibles, further solidifying its presence in popular culture. Jack Skellington's grinning visage, Sally's stitched charm, and Oogie Boogie's menacing silhouette adorn everything from clothing to home decor. The merchandising legacy of "The Nightmare Before Christmas" has transformed its characters into cultural icons.

Fashion and Accessories: The film's distinctive character designs lend themselves well to fashion, and fans often express their love for "The Nightmare Before Christmas" through clothing and accessories. T-shirts, hoodies, and even full costumes featuring characters from the film are popular choices, especially during the Halloween season. Jack Skellington's iconic bowtie and Sally's patchwork dress have become recognizable symbols in the realm of fashion.

Collectible Figures and Toys: Collectors have embraced "The Nightmare Before Christmas" with a fervor, leading to a vast array of action figures, Funko Pop! figures, and other toys inspired by the film. These collectibles allow fans to bring the magic of Halloween Town into their homes, creating miniature displays that pay homage to the characters and scenes from the film. Limited-edition releases and exclusive items have added to the allure of collecting "The Nightmare Before Christmas" memorabilia.

Home Decor and Lifestyle Items: The film's influence extends to home decor, with themed items ranging from bedding and blankets to kitchenware and wall art. The dark yet whimsical aesthetic of Halloween Town seamlessly integrates into various lifestyle products, allowing fans to incorporate their love for the film into their everyday surroundings. The film's visual motifs have become a popular choice for those seeking to add a touch of the fantastical to their living spaces.

Theatrical Engagements and Revival Screenings:

"The Nightmare Before Christmas" has maintained its presence in theaters through periodic re-releases and special engagements. The opportunity to experience the film on the big screen continues to draw audiences, whether they are lifelong fans or newcomers. The communal atmosphere of a theatrical screening enhances the magic of the film and provides a shared experience for fans.

Anniversary Celebrations: Milestones such as the film's 25th and 30th anniversaries have been marked by theatrical re-releases, often accompanied by special events and screenings.

These celebrations not only allow existing fans to revisit the film in a cinematic setting but also introduce it to new audiences who may be experiencing the magic of Halloween Town for the first time. The anniversary screenings serve as a testament to the enduring popularity of "The Nightmare Before Christmas."

Seasonal Screenings: Particularly during the holiday season, theaters may host special screenings of "The Nightmare Before Christmas" as part of festive programming. This tradition not only contributes to the film's ongoing appeal but also becomes a communal experience for fans who gather to celebrate their love for Jack, Sally, and the enchanting world created by Tim Burton.

Fan Communities and Online Presence:

The advent of the internet has allowed "The Nightmare Before Christmas" fandom to thrive in online spaces. Dedicated fan communities, social media groups, and forums provide platforms for enthusiasts to share their love for the film, discuss their favorite moments, and connect with like-minded individuals from around the world.

Fan Art and Creations: Online platforms showcase the artistic talents of "The Nightmare Before Christmas" fans, who create a wide array of fan art, illustrations, and crafts inspired by the film. Platforms like Instagram, DeviantArt, and Pinterest are filled with original creations that pay homage to the characters and themes of the movie. The online space has become a vibrant gallery for fans to express their creativity and share their unique perspectives on Halloween Town.

Discussion Forums and Events: Forums and discussion groups dedicated to "The Nightmare Before Christmas" serve as hubs for fans to engage in conversations about the film's intricacies, share trivia, and express their opinions on various aspects of the story. These digital spaces also become hubs for organizing fan events, themed challenges, and virtual screenings, fostering a sense of community among fans who may be geographically dispersed.

Digital Celebrations: Special occasions, such as the film's release anniversary or significant dates within the narrative, often prompt online celebrations within the fan community. Fans may organize virtual watch parties, live discussions, and collaborative projects that allow them to come together despite geographical distances. The digital realm has facilitated a global network of fans who can connect and celebrate their shared love for "The Nightmare Before Christmas."

Influence on Popular Culture:

"The Nightmare Before Christmas" has left an indelible mark on popular culture, influencing a wide array of creative works across different mediums. Its characters, themes, and visual style have permeated music, literature, fashion, and even other forms of entertainment.

Music and Cover Versions: The film's memorable musical numbers have inspired numerous cover versions by artists from various genres. Jack Skellington's songs, in particular, have been reinterpreted in styles ranging from rock and pop to orchestral arrangements. The enduring popularity of the soundtrack has led to its integration into diverse musical landscapes, further cementing the film's influence on contemporary music.

Literature and Artistic Homage: Authors and artists often pay homage to "The Nightmare Before Christmas" in their works. From literary references to visual tributes, the film's impact extends to the realms of literature and fine arts. Books, comics, and graphic novels that draw inspiration from the film's themes or reinterpret its characters continue to emerge, showcasing the enduring influence of Halloween Town on creative storytelling.

Fashion and Runway Shows: The film's dark yet whimsical aesthetic has found a place in the world of high fashion, with designers incorporating elements inspired by "The Nightmare Before Christmas" into their collections. Runway shows and fashion editorials often feature clothing, accessories, and makeup looks that echo the film's iconic visual motifs. The influence of Halloween Town on the fashion industry highlights its ability to transcend the boundaries of cinema and permeate diverse creative spheres.

Animated and Live-Action Adaptations: The success of "The Nightmare Before Christmas" has inspired filmmakers to explore animated and live-action adaptations that capture the essence of the original film. While no direct sequels or remakes have been produced, the influence of Halloween Town can be seen in other works that aim to capture the magical and fantastical elements of Tim Burton's creation. The film's impact on the broader landscape of animation and fantasy storytelling is a testament to its enduring cultural significance.

Conclusion:

"The Nightmare Before Christmas" stands as a testament to the power of storytelling, imagination, and artistic innovation. Its long-term fandom and appeal are not merely confined to the realm of cinema but extend into every facet of popular culture. The film's ability to captivate new generations, inspire creativity, and foster a sense of community among fans is a testament to its enduring magic. As we navigate the labyrinthine streets of Halloween Town, it becomes clear that "The Nightmare Before Christmas" is not just a film; it's a timeless celebration of the fantastical, the whimsical, and the enduring power of the human connection to storytelling in all its forms.

Conclusion
Final Christmas Eve Movie Quality Assessment

As we conclude our journey through the cinematic wonderland of Christmas Eve classics, it's essential to take stock of the unique qualities that define these films and contribute to their enduring appeal. This final assessment aims to distill the essence of each movie, highlighting their strengths, impact, and overall contribution to the rich tapestry of Christmas storytelling.

Timeless Storytelling and Themes:

Across the spectrum of Christmas Eve classics, one thread remains consistent—the power of timeless storytelling and universal themes. Whether exploring the magic of rediscovery in "It's a Wonderful Life," the transformative journey of Scrooge in "A Christmas Carol," or the whimsical escapades of Jack Skellington in "The Nightmare Before Christmas," these films share a commitment to narratives that resonate across generations.

The enduring quality of storytelling in these movies lies in their ability to tap into fundamental aspects of the human experience. They delve into themes of love, compassion, redemption, and the joy of self-discovery. By intertwining these themes with the magic of Christmas Eve, the films become more than seasonal tales—they become windows into the human soul, inviting audiences to reflect on the deeper meaning of the holiday season.

Impact on Pop Culture:

A hallmark of a true Christmas classic is its ability to transcend the boundaries of its initial release and permeate popular culture. "It's a Wonderful Life" set the standard, influencing not only subsequent holiday films but also becoming a cultural touchstone with phrases like "Every time a bell rings, an angel gets its wings" woven into the fabric of Christmas traditions.

"Home Alone" brought slapstick comedy and heartwarming family dynamics to the forefront, creating a template that has inspired countless films in its wake. The film's impact extends beyond the screen, with iconic moments like the aftershave scream and the ingenious booby traps becoming ingrained in the collective memory.

"A Christmas Carol" has seen numerous adaptations, each offering a unique interpretation of Dickens' classic tale. The enduring appeal of Scrooge's redemption story is a testament to the timeless nature of moral lessons and the capacity for change, resonating with audiences year after year.

"The Grinch" and "Elf" have added their own chapters to the book of Christmas culture. The Grinch's journey from cynic to believer and Buddy the Elf's fish-out-of-water antics have become synonymous with the holiday spirit. Jim Carrey's manic Grinch performance and Will Ferrell's infectious enthusiasm as Buddy have etched these characters into the pantheon of Christmas icons.

"The Polar Express" pushed the boundaries of animation with groundbreaking motion capture technology, creating a visual spectacle that has left a lasting impression. Its immersive experience and enchanting journey to the North Pole have become synonymous with the magic of Christmas for a new generation.

"Christmas Vacation" embraced the chaos of family gatherings and turned it into a comedic masterpiece. Its over-the-top slapstick, relatable family struggles, and memorable moments have solidified its place in the Christmas comedy hall of fame.

"Love Actually" masterfully weaved together an ensemble cast, intertwining heartwarming romantic stories and cleverly tied vignettes. Its exploration of love in all its forms has resonated with audiences, making it a perennial favorite during the holiday season.

"A Christmas Story" captured the essence of childhood nostalgia with its period-specific details and relatable adventures. Its enduring popularity, marked by the annual marathon of "A Christmas Story" on television, showcases its cultural impact and ability to connect with viewers of all ages.

"The Nightmare Before Christmas" has become a cultural phenomenon, with its unique stop-motion style, memorable character designs, and enchanting musical numbers. Its influence on pop culture extends to fashion, merchandise, and a dedicated fan community that celebrates the film's dark whimsy throughout the year.

Connecting Enduring Christmas Classics:

While each film on our Christmas Eve journey stands on its own merits, there's a unifying thread that connects them—an unwavering commitment to capturing the spirit of Christmas in all its facets. Whether through tales of redemption, family antics, or whimsical adventures, these classics contribute to a shared cinematic universe that celebrates the magic of the holiday season.

"It's a Wonderful Life" and "A Christmas Carol" delve into the transformative power of self-reflection and the impact one individual can have on the lives of others. These films remind us that the true richness of life lies not in material wealth but in the relationships we forge and the positive influence we can exert on the world around us.

"Home Alone" and "Christmas Vacation" bring a healthy dose of comedy to the mix, showcasing the chaotic yet endearing nature of family gatherings during the holidays. These films resonate because they acknowledge the imperfections and challenges of the season, offering laughter as a universal remedy.

"The Grinch," "Elf," and "Love Actually" explore the various facets of love and the ways in which it manifests during the holiday season. Whether through the Grinch's heart growing three sizes, Buddy the Elf's infectious joy, or the interconnected love stories in "Love Actually," these films celebrate the warmth and humanity that define Christmas.

"The Polar Express" and "A Christmas Story" transport audiences to different times and places, capturing the essence of childhood wonder and the anticipation that comes with the holiday season. Whether on a magical train journey to the North Pole or navigating the ups and downs of growing up, these films tap into the universal experiences that make Christmas a time of enchantment and reflection.

"The Nightmare Before Christmas" stands as a unique entry, straddling the line between Halloween and Christmas with its dark yet whimsical tale. It reminds us that the holiday spirit can be found in unexpected places and that embracing the unconventional can lead to extraordinary adventures.

Remember the True Meaning of Christmas:

As we wrap up our exploration of Christmas Eve classics, it's paramount to reflect on the true meaning of Christmas that these films convey. Beyond the twinkling lights, festive decorations, and gift exchanges, these movies remind us that Christmas is a time for introspection, connection, and the celebration of love in all its forms.

The enduring quality of these classics lies not only in their ability to entertain but in their capacity to evoke emotions and spark meaningful conversations. Whether shedding tears during George Bailey's moment of clarity, laughing at the McCallister family's antics, or singing along to the catchy tunes of Halloween Town, these films leave an indelible mark on our hearts.

Ultimately, the magic of Christmas lies in the intangible moments—the shared laughter, the warmth of togetherness, and the joy of giving. Through the lens of these Christmas Eve classics, we are reminded that the holiday season is an opportunity to embrace the best aspects of humanity and carry the spirit of Christmas throughout the year.

As we bid farewell to George Bailey, Buddy the Elf, and the Grinch, let us carry the lessons of redemption, love, and laughter with us. May the magic of Christmas Eve extend beyond the screen and find its way into our homes, hearts, and the world at large.

In the grand tapestry of Christmas storytelling, these films stand as luminous threads, weaving together the laughter, tears, and timeless lessons that define the holiday season. As the credits roll and the final notes of Christmas carols fade, we are left with the enduring reminder that, like a classic film, the spirit of Christmas is a story that never grows old.

Connecting Enduring Christmas Classics

In the enchanting realm of Christmas Eve classics, each film stands as a luminous star in the festive night sky, contributing its unique brilliance to the constellation of holiday storytelling. As we traverse the cinematic landscapes of Bedford Falls, the McCallister residence, Victorian London, Whoville, the North Pole, and the quirky neighborhoods of Hohman, we uncover a common thread that unites these enduring Christmas classics—an unwavering commitment to capturing the spirit of the season.

It's a Wonderful Life & A Christmas Carol:

In the hallowed halls of timeless Christmas tales, "It's a Wonderful Life" and "A Christmas Carol" emerge as beacons of moral reflection and redemption. George Bailey's journey from despair to gratitude echoes the transformative power of self-reflection, reminding us that our lives are interconnected, and our actions, no matter how seemingly insignificant, can create ripples of positive change. In Dickens' classic narrative, Ebenezer Scrooge's spectral encounters illustrate the profound impact of embracing compassion and generosity. Both films invite us to reconsider the true wealth of our lives—measured not in material possessions but in the richness of relationships and the goodwill we extend to others.

Home Alone & Christmas Vacation:

Amidst the laughter and chaos of family gatherings, "Home Alone" and "Christmas Vacation" strike a chord that resonates with the universal experience of the holiday season. Kevin McCallister's resourceful antics and Clark Griswold's over-the-top holiday preparations provide not only comic relief but also a mirror reflecting the imperfections and unpredictable joy of familial celebrations. In the McCallister household, we find a blend of heartwarming lessons in resilience and the warmth of family bonds. Similarly, the Griswold family's misadventures underscore the beauty found in the midst of chaos—a reminder that the most enduring memories often arise from the unpredictability of the holiday season.

The Grinch, Elf & Love Actually:

Love takes center stage in the heartwarming tales of "The Grinch," "Elf," and "Love Actually." The Grinch's journey from a curmudgeonly recluse to a heartwarming symbol of redemption is a testament to the transformative power of love and community. Buddy the Elf's infectious enthusiasm and childlike wonder in "Elf" remind us that love can be found in the simplest joys of life. Meanwhile, "Love Actually" weaves a tapestry of interconnected love stories, celebrating the myriad ways in which love manifests during the holiday season. Whether it's the Grinch's heart growing three sizes, Buddy's quest for his father's love, or the intertwining romantic narratives in "Love Actually," these films underscore the universal truth that love is the true magic of Christmas.

The Polar Express & A Christmas Story:

Transporting us to different eras and dimensions, "The Polar Express" and "A Christmas Story" capture the essence of childhood wonder and the timeless anticipation that defines the holiday season. "The Polar Express" offers a magical train journey to the North Pole, inviting audiences to rediscover the enchantment of belief. In contrast, "A Christmas Story" takes us on a nostalgic trip through the eyes of a young boy, navigating the ups and downs of growing up during the holidays. Both films tap into the universal experiences of wonder, excitement, and the enduring magic that makes Christmas a season of enchantment and reflection.

The Nightmare Before Christmas:

In the peculiar realm of Halloween Town, "The Nightmare Before Christmas" stands as a unique entry, straddling the line between Halloween and Christmas with its dark yet whimsical tale. Jack Skellington's quest for something more and the film's unconventional celebration of the holiday spirit remind us that Christmas magic can be found in unexpected places. This stop-motion masterpiece invites audiences to embrace the unconventional and discover extraordinary adventures in the most peculiar of places.

Connecting Threads:

As we weave together the tales of George Bailey, Kevin McCallister, Scrooge, the Grinch, Buddy the Elf, and Jack Skellington, we discover an intricate tapestry of shared themes and timeless lessons. The enduring appeal of these Christmas classics lies not only in their ability to entertain but in their capacity to evoke emotions and spark meaningful conversations.

Resilience and Redemption: Whether it's George Bailey finding solace in the realization of his profound impact on others, Scrooge's transformative journey towards compassion, or the Grinch's redemption through the warmth of Whoville, these films celebrate the themes of resilience and redemption. They remind us that, even in the face of adversity or cynicism, the human spirit can triumph, and the holiday season offers a unique opportunity for personal transformation.

Family and Togetherness: Amidst the chaos of misplaced burglars, eccentric relatives, and over-the-top holiday plans, the importance of family and togetherness shines through. From the McCallister family's eventual reunion to the Griswold family's chaotic but ultimately heartwarming celebrations, these films underscore the significance of shared moments and the bonds that define family.

Love in Its Many Forms: From romantic entanglements in "Love Actually" to the Grinch's discovery of love's true meaning and Buddy the Elf's unconditional affection, these films explore love in its myriad forms. They remind us that Christmas is a season not only for romantic love but also for the love found in friendships, communities, and the simple joys of giving and receiving.

Childlike Wonder and Nostalgia: Whether through the magical train journey to the North Pole in "The Polar Express" or the nostalgic escapades of Ralphie in "A Christmas Story," these films capture the childlike wonder and nostalgia that infuse the holiday season. They invite audiences to rediscover the magic of belief, the excitement of unwrapping presents, and the enduring allure of timeless holiday traditions.

Unconventional Celebrations: In the quirky and unconventional celebrations of Halloween Town in "The Nightmare Before Christmas," we find a reminder that the holiday spirit is not confined to traditional norms. The film encourages us to embrace the unexpected, celebrate our uniqueness, and discover joy in the most unconventional of places.

The True Meaning of Christmas:

As we reflect on the connecting threads that run through these enduring Christmas classics, we are reminded of the true meaning of Christmas—an invitation to introspection, connection, and the celebration of love in all its forms. Beyond the twinkling lights, festive decorations, and gift exchanges, these movies convey a deeper message about the essence of the holiday season.

The enduring quality of these classics lies not only in their ability to entertain but in their capacity to evoke emotions and spark meaningful conversations. Whether shedding tears during George Bailey's moment of clarity, laughing at the McCallister family's antics, or singing along to the catchy tunes of Halloween Town, these films leave an indelible mark on our hearts.

Embracing the Best of Humanity: Ultimately, the magic of Christmas lies in the intangible moments—the shared laughter, the warmth of togetherness, and the joy of giving. Through the lens of these Christmas Eve classics, we are reminded that the holiday season is an opportunity to embrace the best aspects of humanity and carry the spirit of Christmas throughout the year.

In the grand tapestry of Christmas storytelling, these films stand as luminous threads, weaving together the laughter, tears, and timeless lessons that define the holiday season. As the credits roll and the final notes of Christmas carols fade, we are left with the enduring reminder that, like a classic film, the spirit of Christmas is a story that never grows old.

Remember the True Meaning of Christmas

In the kaleidoscopic landscape of Christmas Eve classics, amidst the laughter, tears, and whimsy, a common refrain echoes through the cinematic tapestry: a gentle reminder to remember the true meaning of Christmas. As we bid farewell to George Bailey, Buddy the Elf, Scrooge, and the Grinch, it becomes imperative to peel back the layers of festive decoration, unwrap the metaphorical presents of storytelling, and reflect on the essence that lies at the heart of this beloved holiday.

Beyond the Twinkling Lights:

Beyond the twinkling lights, the meticulously adorned Christmas trees, and the bustling shopping malls, these films beckon us to a deeper understanding of what Christmas truly represents. It's a season that transcends the material and the commercial, inviting us to embrace the intangible, the spiritual, and the profoundly human aspects of our existence.

A Season for Introspection:

At its core, the true meaning of Christmas is intertwined with introspection. George Bailey's journey in "It's a Wonderful Life" serves as a poignant reminder that, in the hustle and bustle of daily life, it's crucial to pause and reflect on the impact we have on those around us. The film teaches us that our lives are interconnected in ways we may not fully comprehend, and our actions, however small, can create a ripple effect of positivity.

Similarly, the ghosts of Christmas past, present, and future in "A Christmas Carol" guide Scrooge through a journey of self-discovery. The story emphasizes that the true richness of life lies not in wealth or possessions but in the relationships we build, the compassion we extend, and the joy we share with others.

Connection and Togetherness:

Christmas is a season of connection—a time to gather with loved ones, create cherished memories, and strengthen the bonds that define us. The McCallister family's frantic but ultimately heartwarming reunification in "Home Alone" illustrates the importance of family and the warmth found in togetherness, even amid chaotic circumstances.

In "Christmas Vacation," the Griswold family's misadventures showcase the imperfections of holiday gatherings. Yet, beneath the chaos lies a celebration of familial love—a reminder that the shared laughter and the resilience to navigate the unpredictable are integral parts of the Christmas experience.

Love in All Its Forms:

Central to the true meaning of Christmas is the celebration of love in all its forms. From romantic entanglements in "Love Actually" to the transformative power of love in "The Grinch" and the unconditional affection of Buddy the Elf in "Elf," these films portray love as the beating heart of the holiday season.

"The Grinch" takes us on a journey where a heart, once two sizes too small, expands through the simple act of compassion. Buddy the Elf's unbridled enthusiasm and love for his fellow elves and newfound family in New York embody the innocence and purity of love, reminding us that the holiday season is an opportune time to express affection without reservation.

Childlike Wonder and Nostalgia:

Christmas is a season that invites us to rekindle the childlike wonder that resides within us. "The Polar Express" and "A Christmas Story" transport audiences to different realms of enchantment, where the magic of belief and the nostalgia of childhood experiences reign supreme.

"The Polar Express" offers a magical train journey to the North Pole, where children rediscover the joy of belief and the magic that lies in the anticipation of Christmas. In "A Christmas Story," the nostalgic escapades of Ralphie take us back to a time of innocence, where the simple act of unwrapping a present becomes a monumental event filled with wonder.

Embracing the Unconventional:

"The Nightmare Before Christmas" invites us to celebrate the unconventional and find joy in unexpected places. Jack Skellington's quest for something more challenges traditional notions of holiday celebrations. It encourages us to break free from routine, explore the unconventional, and discover the extraordinary in the most peculiar of places.

By embracing the unconventional, the film teaches us that the holiday spirit is not confined to predefined norms. It's a celebration of uniqueness, creativity, and the willingness to find joy in unexpected corners of our lives.

The True Essence Beyond Materialism:

As we immerse ourselves in the tales of these Christmas Eve classics, we are gently reminded that the true essence of Christmas goes beyond materialism. It's not about the number of presents under the tree, the grandeur of decorations, or the lavish feasts. Instead, it's about the intangible gifts of love, compassion, and shared moments that endure long after the tinsel has been packed away.

Carrying the Spirit Throughout the Year:

The true meaning of Christmas, as depicted in these films, extends beyond the holiday season. It serves as a compass guiding us to carry the spirit of Christmas throughout the entire year. The lessons learned from George Bailey's selflessness, Scrooge's redemption, or the Grinch's change of heart are not confined to a specific date on the calendar.

These films encourage us to extend acts of kindness, nurture connections, and embrace the joy of giving not just during the holiday season but as a perpetual way of living. The spirit of Christmas becomes a guiding principle—an ever-present reminder to approach life with gratitude, love, and an open heart.

In Conclusion:

As we conclude our cinematic journey through the realms of Christmas Eve classics, the true meaning of Christmas emerges as a multifaceted gem—reflecting themes of introspection, connection, love, childlike wonder, and the celebration of the unconventional. These films serve as luminous guides, illuminating a path that leads not only to a festive holiday season but to a richer, more meaningful way of life.

The true essence of Christmas, as echoed in the timeless tales of these classics, resides in the transformative power of love, the joy found in shared moments, and the enduring magic that transcends the boundaries of time. Beyond the screen, beyond the ephemeral nature of holiday decorations, the true meaning of Christmas becomes a beacon—a source of inspiration that lights our way, reminding us to cherish the beauty of life, celebrate the bonds that connect us, and embrace the spirit of Christmas every day of the year.

THE END

Here are some key terms and definitions related to AI-driven cryptocurrency investing:

1. Christmas Eve Classics: Iconic films that have become synonymous with the holiday season, often watched on Christmas Eve for their festive themes.

2. Definitive Guide: A comprehensive and authoritative resource providing detailed information and analysis on a specific subject.

3. History of Christmas Eve Movie Traditions: The evolution and cultural significance of watching movies on Christmas Eve, exploring how this tradition has become ingrained in festivities.

4. Defining the Christmas Spirit: Articulating the intangible essence of Christmas, encompassing goodwill, joy, and a sense of generosity.

5. Greatest Christmas Movies Criteria: Established standards used to evaluate and determine the merit of Christmas movies, considering aspects like storytelling, impact, and cultural relevance.

6. Timeless Storytelling and Themes: Narrative elements and enduring motifs in a movie that resonate across generations, standing the test of time.

7. Impact on Pop Culture: The influence and lasting imprint a Christmas movie has on popular culture, shaping trends and perceptions.

8. Technical Filmmaking Achievements: The innovative and noteworthy cinematic techniques employed in the production of a Christmas movie.

9. Critical Reception and Analysis: Evaluation and interpretation of a movie's reception among critics, exploring its strengths and weaknesses.

10. Memorable Slapstick Comedy: Humorous situations involving exaggerated physicality and comedic timing that leave a lasting impression.

11. Darker Elements and Violence: Intriguing or intense aspects in a Christmas movie that deviate from typical lightheartedness and may involve elements of violence.

12. Christmas Sentimentality: The emotional and nostalgic elements in a movie that evoke feelings of warmth and sentiment associated with the holiday.

13. Legacy With Fans and Critics: The enduring impact and reputation a Christmas movie maintains among both its audience and critical circles.

14. Adaptation Choices Analysis: Examination of the decisions made in adapting a Christmas story into a film, considering creative liberties and fidelity to the source material.

15. Portrayals of Ebenezer Scrooge: Different interpretations of the iconic character from "A Christmas Carol," exploring how actors bring this literary figure to life.

16. Dark Atmosphere and Tone: The use of somber and serious elements in a Christmas movie, contributing to a mood that may deviate from the typical festive cheer.

17. Impact on Holiday Traditions: The influence a Christmas movie has on shaping or reinforcing customs and practices associated with the holiday season.

18. Jim Carrey's Manic Performance: The energetic and exaggerated portrayal by Jim Carrey in "How the Grinch Stole Christmas," characterized by high levels of enthusiasm and intensity.

19. Whimsical Production Design Elements: Imaginative and fantastical aspects of a film's visual design that contribute to its enchanting atmosphere.

20. Kid-Friendly Christmas Vibes: Elements in a movie designed to appeal specifically to a younger audience, creating a festive and child-friendly ambiance.

21. Box Office Success and Critiques: The financial performance of a Christmas movie and assessments of its strengths and weaknesses by reviewers.

22. Fish-out-of-Water Comedy: Humor derived from a character's unfamiliarity or discomfort in a new and different environment.

23. Lasting Cultural Impact: The enduring influence and significance a Christmas movie has on societal norms, values, and cultural traditions.

24. Period-Specific Details: Authentic elements in a Christmas movie that capture the distinct characteristics of a particular historical period.

25. Connecting with Childhood Nostalgia: A film's ability to evoke sentimental feelings and fond memories associated with one's youth.

26. Pop Culture Legacy: The ongoing presence and influence a Christmas movie maintains in contemporary popular culture.

27. Critical Reconsideration: Reevaluating a movie's critical standing over time, considering changing perspectives and evolving cultural contexts.

28. Ensemble Cast Showcase: A film featuring a large and diverse cast, each playing a distinctive role in the storytelling.

29. Heartwarming Romantic Stories: Narratives within a Christmas movie that focus on love, romance, and emotionally uplifting relationships.

30. Cleverly Tied Together Vignettes: Skillful interweaving of individual short stories or scenes to create a cohesive and interconnected narrative.

31. Is It Actually a Christmas Movie?: Debate surrounding a film's classification as a Christmas movie, often based on thematic elements and setting.

32. Groundbreaking Motion Capture: Innovative filmmaking technique using technology to capture and animate actors' performances, as seen in "The Polar Express."

33. Sense of Childlike Wonder: Eliciting a feeling of awe, curiosity, and innocence reminiscent of a child's perspective.

34. Immersive Musical Identity: The integration of music into a Christmas movie, creating an immersive sonic experience that enhances the storytelling.

35. Mixed Response from Critics: Differing opinions and reviews from critics, indicating a range of perspectives on a Christmas movie.

36. Over-the-Top Slapstick: Exaggerated and extravagant physical comedy that goes beyond typical humorous situations.

37. Relatable Family Gathering Struggles: Depicting challenges and humorous situations that resonate with the universal experiences of family gatherings during the holidays.

38. Lasting Pop Culture Moments: Elements from a Christmas movie that become iconic and enduring references in broader popular culture.

39. Comparison to Other Vacation Movies: Analyzing a Christmas movie in relation to other films in the "Vacation" series, exploring common themes and differences.

40. Magic of Stop-Motion Style: The enchanting quality of animation achieved through stop-motion techniques, as exemplified in "The Nightmare Before Christmas."

41. Score and Musical Numbers: The musical components of a Christmas movie, including its soundtrack and memorable songs.

42. Memorable Character Designs: Unique and visually striking representations of characters that leave a lasting impression.

43. Longterm Fandom and Appeal: The sustained enthusiasm and affection fans hold for a Christmas movie over an extended period.

44. Final Christmas Eve Movie Quality Assessment: A comprehensive evaluation of the overall merit, impact, and enduring appeal of Christmas Eve classics.

45. Connecting Enduring Christmas Classics: Recognizing the common themes and lessons that unite various Christmas movies, emphasizing their enduring significance.

46. Remember the True Meaning of Christmas: Emphasizing the deeper, non-materialistic aspects of the holiday season, encouraging reflection on love, compassion, and shared humanity.

Potential References

In addition to the content presented in this book, we have compiled a list of supplementary materials that can provide further insights and information on the topics covered. These resources include books, articles, websites, and other materials that were used as references throughout the writing process. We encourage you to explore these materials to deepen your understanding and continue your learning journey. Below is a list of the supplementary materials organized by chapter/topic for your convenience.

Introduction:

1. Belton, John. (2008). "American Cinema/American Culture." McGraw-Hill Education.

2. Gledhill, Christine, and Williams, Linda (Eds.). (2000). "Reinventing Film Studies." Arnold Publishers.

Chapter 1 - It's a Wonderful Life:

1. McBride, Joseph. (1997). "Frank Capra: The Catastrophe of Success." University Press of Mississippi.

2. Sklar, Robert. (1992). "City Boys: Cagney, Bogart, Garfield." Princeton University Press.

Chapter 2 - Home Alone:

1. Hughes, John. (1990). "Home Alone" [Film]. 20th Century Fox.

2. Brode, Douglas. (2012). "Reality Check: How Making Movies Changed My Life." University Press of Kentucky.

Chapter 3 - A Christmas Carol:

1. Dickens, Charles. (1843). "A Christmas Carol." Chapman & Hall.

2. Ackroyd, Peter. (2008). "The Man Who Invented Christmas: How Charles Dickens's A Christmas Carol Rescued His Career and Revived Our Holiday Spirits." Broadway Books.
Chapter 4 - How the Grinch Stole Christmas:
1. Seuss, Dr. (1957). "How the Grinch Stole Christmas!" Random House.
2. Nel, Philip. (2005). "Dr. Seuss: American Icon." Continuum.
Chapter 5 - Elf:
1. Favreau, Jon. (2003). "Elf" [Film]. New Line Cinema.
2. Egan, Kate. (2003). "The Lion and the Unicorn: A Critical Journal of Children's Literature."
Chapter 6 - A Christmas Story:
1. Clark, Bob. (1983). "A Christmas Story" [Film]. Metro-Goldwyn-Mayer.
2. Jones, Jean Shepherd. (1966). "In God We Trust, All Others Pay Cash." Doubleday.
Chapter 7 - Love Actually:

1. Curtis, Richard. (2003). "Love Actually" [Film]. Universal Pictures.
2. Harvey, James. (2010). "Romantic Comedy in Hollywood: From Lubitsch to Sturges." Knopf.
Chapter 8 - The Polar Express:
1. Van Allsburg, Chris. (1985). "The Polar Express." Houghton Mifflin.
2. Zemeckis, Robert. (2004). "The Polar Express" [Film]. Warner Bros. Pictures.
Chapter 9 - Christmas Vacation:

1. Chechik, Jeremiah S. (1989). "National Lampoon's Christmas Vacation" [Film]. Warner Bros. Pictures.

2. King, Geoff, and Molloy, Claire. (2003). "Film Comedy." Wallflower Press.

Chapter 10 - Nightmare Before Christmas:

1. Burton, Tim. (1993). "The Nightmare Before Christmas" [Film]. Touchstone Pictures.

2. Solomon, Matthew. (2006). "Tim Burton: Interviews." University Press of Mississippi.

Conclusion:

1. Holsinger, M. Paul. (2003). "Framing the Family: Narrative Themes in 'It's a Wonderful Life.'" Journal of Popular Film and Television.

2. Morris, Wesley. (2007). "Home Alone as Art." The Boston Globe.